THE MODERN APPLIQUÉ WORKBOOK

- Easy Invisible Zigzag Method
- 11 Quilts to Round Out Your Skills

JENIFER DICK

stashBOOKS.

an imprint of C&T Publishing

Text copyright © 2013 by Jenifer Dick

Photography and Artwork copyright © 2013 by C&T Publishing, Inc.

Publisher: Amy Marson

Creative Director: Gailen Runge

Art Director/Cover Designer: Kristy Zacharias

Editor: Deb Rowden

Technical Editors: Sandy Peterson and Julie Waldman

Book Designer: April Mostek

Production Coordinator: Zinnia Heinzmann

Production Editors: Alice Mace Nakanishi and Katie Van Amburg

Illustrator: Jessica Jenkins

Photo Assistant: Mary Peyton Peppo

Photography by Diane Pedersen and Nissa Brehmer of C&T Publishing, Inc., unless otherwise noted

Published by Stash Books, an imprint of C&T Publishing, Inc., P.O. Box 1456, Lafayette, CA 94549

Library of Congress Cataloging-in-Publication Data

Dick, Jenifer.

 The modern appliqué workbook : easy invisible zigzag method--11 quilts to round out your skills / Jenifer Dick.

   pages cm

 ISBN 978-1-60705-763-5 (soft cover)

 1. Machine appliqué. 2. Machine quilting. 3. Quilts. I. Title.

 TT779.D49 2013

 746.44'5--dc23

                        2013018218

Printed in China

10 9 8 7 6 5 4 3 2 1

Dedication

For Ray

Acknowledgments

This book couldn't have been written without the help of some very special and generous people.

To Angela Walters, thank you for adding your expert quilting to my quilt designs. Your unique eye and artistry made these quilts more beautiful than I could have ever imagined.

To Jaime David and the staff of Bernina Sewing Center of Kansas City, thank you for sharing both your expertise and machines with me.

To the staff at Stash Books, thank you for allowing me to write the book I've always wanted to write. And to my editor, Deb, thanks for talking me down off the cliff more than once!

And to my wonderful family, thank you for helping me to pursue my goal in writing this book even though it meant long hours in the sewing room and on the computer away from you. I love you!

Contents

INTRODUCTION:
My Journey to Modern Appliqué

When I first started quiltmaking in the early 1990s, appliqué seemed so daunting. My first attempts at hand appliqué didn't go well—it was slower than I wanted, and I just couldn't get the stitches perfected so they didn't show. I experimented with fusible web appliqué, but it didn't give me the look or durability I was going for. Soon, I went out of my way to avoid appliqué patterns and accepted that it just wasn't a technique for me.

As time passed, I advanced in my piecing skills but still admired lovely appliqué quilts that I thought I would never be able to make. Then a few years later, I saw a demonstration at a guild meeting that finally clicked with me. The instructor showed us how to prepare appliqué shapes using freezer paper. I had never seen that method before and didn't even really know what freezer paper was at the time. It intrigued me so much that I stopped by the store on the way home to buy freezer paper and gluesticks. It was one of those light bulb moments—I knew I had found something I could make work for me!

Once I perfected the shape-making method, it was on to the sewing machine and stitches. I don't remember how the teacher sewed the shapes down—I think it involved a lot of changing threads in colors to match the appliqué shapes. I didn't have a big stash of thread at that time and didn't want to invest in a lot of thread colors I might never use up, so instead I started experimenting with invisible polyester thread. It glides through the machine just like cotton thread and winds on the bobbin with little effort. But most of all, with it I could easily create perfect machine appliqué blocks that mimic fine hand appliqué!

That was in 2001. With the advent of modern quilting, I've come to realize mimicking hand appliqué isn't always the best choice, it's just one of many best choices. Just as modern piecing focuses on a fresh and fun design aesthetic, so does modern machine appliqué. That can mean using a wide variety of stitches, threads, and unusual subject matter to create appliqué. How you sew the shape down and what you use to do so become part of the visual appeal of the design itself, not just a means to attach the shape to the block.

In this book you'll find instructions, tips, and hints for the Invisible Zigzag Appliqué method from start to finish. After you learn the basic method, you can move on to learn more techniques and options, advanced preparation steps, and ideas for finishing appliqué quilts. Eleven projects are included for you to practice your new skills on.

My goal is that after you've made a few of your own appliqué blocks using this method, you'll realize how attainable perfect machine appliqué is. And then I hope you'll experiment with all the tools available to you to take an active role in defining what modern appliqué can be—as only modern quilters can do—with no excuses and no apologies!

The Modern Appliqué Workbook

The Modern Appliqué
WORKBOOK

PART I: Invisible Zigzag Appliqué

Once you master the Invisible Zigzag Appliqué technique, you will have a go-to machine appliqué method that works consistently and beautifully every time. There are several steps to both preparing the freezer paper and sewing the shapes down, but you'll find that they are intuitive and easy to follow. The end results will be the proof! My methods are described in this section, and you'll find them applied to the eleven projects that follow.

Tools and Supplies

Having the right tools is as important as knowing the right techniques—the tools make the appliqué experience more fun and less stressful. This book assumes you have a basic knowledge of quiltmaking and its terminology and you already have basic quilt-making supplies on hand. However, there are some tools specific to appliqué that you'll need for Invisible Zigzag Appliqué.

This list includes my favorite tools and supplies. Some of these might already be in your home. Read through the list before you make any purchases—you might be able to get by without some of the things listed or be able to improvise with something else. Experiment to see what works best for you and your sewing machine.

A FREEZER PAPER

Freezer paper is a thick paper with a shiny, plastic coating on one side. Its original use is wrapping food for storage in the freezer, but it's also a versatile crafting tool. Its paper side is perfect to trace a pattern onto. The shiny side acts like glue and sticks to fabric when pressed with a dry iron. It is repositionable and reusable, inexpensive, and available everywhere. It comes in large rolls, so you can cut off exactly what you need as you need it.

In addition to appliqué, I use freezer paper to make templates for piecing, and I draw original patterns on it. It is 18″ wide, perfect for most block sizes. You can draw on it with a black marker without fear that marks will soak through to the worktable underneath. Overall, it's one of my favorite quilting supplies.

B WATER-SOLUBLE GLUESTICK

Gluesticks are used to glue down the seam allowance on the appliqué shape. Next to freezer paper, you'll use gluesticks the most, so it's important to find a brand that works well for you.

Gluesticks are inexpensive and available anywhere office supplies are sold. But they are not all created equal—look for sticks that are clear and washable.

Try several different brands until you find one you like. You'll quickly discover a preference for a certain brand. Once you find one that works for you, buy the largest size and quantity you can. I've been known to buy cases of gluesticks at a time.

NOTE *There are many colored or "disappearing" gluesticks. I'd be leery of those—they may disappear at first, but it's possible that the color will come back once heat from the iron hits it. If you only have access to colored gluesticks, experiment on a practice block first to see if it will give you satisfactory results.*

C WHITE SCHOOL GLUE

Once the appliqué shapes are prepared, they are glued to the background fabric with white school glue. For this step, you need the smallest amount of glue that is sufficient to tack the shape to the background fabric. You may find the bottle that the school glue comes in has a hole too big and releases too much glue. A needle-nose applicator bottle works well to dole out just the right amount of glue.

NOTE *I like Roxanne Glue-Baste-It because the squeeze bottle has a needle-nose applicator, which allows you to place a tiny dot precisely on the seam allowance. Once the bottle is empty, I refill it with white glue. You can also find empty needle-nose squeeze bottles in the fly-fishing department of outdoor supply stores.*

D CLEAR INVISIBLE POLYESTER THREAD

Invisible polyester thread has many advantages for Invisible Zigzag Appliqué. It's pliable enough to stitch like cotton thread. It won't yellow over time, and it will wind on the bobbin. It blends with all fabrics, making time-consuming thread changes to match the appliqué shapes unnecessary. Most of all, it disappears when sewn, giving the look of hand appliqué.

There are many brands of invisible thread, but I only use Sulky Premier Invisible. It gives me the results I want and works with my sewing machine. Superior Threads MonoPoly is also a good brand and works similarly. Some machines are more finicky than others when it comes to invisible threads. If you are having trouble, I recommend trying a different brand of thread. Nine times out of ten, switching to a different thread takes care of any problems you might be having.

Smoke invisible thread: Invisible thread comes in clear and smoke—clear for use with light fabrics and smoke for dark fabrics. I use clear for everything, though, with the only exception being black appliqué shapes. Even on the darkest reds, clear invisible thread blends well for me.

Regular cotton, polyester, nylon, and other threads: For a review of these threads, see Thread (page 45).

E SEWING MACHINE

At a minimum, all you need is a machine in good working order with a zigzag stitch. A machine with a variety of decorative stitches gives you many more options, but they are not necessary. You can do a lot of fine work with just a straight stitch and a zigzag stitch. I sew on a 30-year-old Bernina 930. It doesn't have all the bells and whistles of a modern machine, but it's a solid machine that gets the job done. Whatever machine you have, keep it serviced and oiled, and it will make a lot of beautiful quilts for you!

Open-toe appliqué foot: This isn't necessary, but it is helpful to be able to see clearly where you're going as you sew. If you don't have one, use a regular zigzag foot first to see if you can work with it. If you decide you need more visibility, look into purchasing an open-toe foot.

F SIZE 80/12 SHARP NEEDLE

When stitching appliqué, the needle goes through three layers of fabric (the background, seam allowance, and top of the shape) as well as the freezer paper. It needs to be sharp to go through all these layers. Sharp needles are also called microtex. Change the needle often for best results.

G SPRAY STARCH

Machine appliqué needs some kind of stabilizer on the background fabric to keep the stitches from bunching as they are sewn. Rather than using a sew-in or tear-away stabilizer, I use spray starch on the background fabric. Starch offers different levels of stiffness to the background, depending on how much or how little you use. It holds its shape and washes out, leaving no residue and eliminating the step of taking out a stabilizer after sewing.

You can use any spray starch you prefer. I mix my own spray starch in a spray bottle using about half starch concentrate (found in the laundry aisle of the grocery store) and half water. I can control the amount of starch I apply to the background with my own mix, and I find it doesn't clog up the spray bottle or flake as easily as commercial spray starch.

H DRY IRON

If you normally use the steam setting on your iron, be sure to empty the water before you begin this type of appliqué. Steam distorts the fabric and wrinkles the freezer paper. You'll get the best results with a dry iron.

OTHER SUPPLIES

- Pencil

- Stapler

- Scissors: a pair for cutting paper, a pair for fabric, *and* a small sharp pair for clipping inner curves

- Stiletto (*optional*) to aid in preparing the shapes and sewing them down. I prefer an orange stick found in the health and beauty department at the grocery store. Its real use is for cleaning fingernails and pushing back cuticles, but its beveled edge works well to turn a seam allowance under and hold a shape down when sewing. It's made of lightweight wood, so if you accidentally sew into it, it won't break a needle or jam your machine.

- Tweezers

- Terry cloth bath towel

- Spray bottle with clean tap water (*optional*)

Fabrics for Appliqué

Any fabric is fair game for appliqué, but each has its own personality and reacts differently. Here are some things to keep in mind when collecting appliqué fabrics.

A COTTON

Quilt shop–quality, 100% cotton fabric is the best choice for piecing, and the same is true for appliqué. It won't ravel, stretch, distort, or fade like lesser fabrics can. You'll get consistent results and be happier with your finished projects. And although the cost of quality fabrics keeps going up, the good news is that you need very little for appliqué. The tiniest of scraps is often all you need, making your fabric stash stretch farther.

B NONCOTTONS OR COTTON BLENDS

Silks, polyesters, ginghams, and other fabrics that are not quilter's cotton all have their own personalities and respond to this method of appliqué differently. Thin fabrics might need to be backed with a lightweight fusible stabilizer to make them sturdier, while others might be too unruly to lie flat without warping or stretching.

Before committing to a lot of work with these fabrics, test them on a sample block to see how they work. If you find them too difficult to work with, don't use them. Instead, look for a similar cotton fabric to substitute.

C BATIKS

Batiks are tightly woven and work fine for appliqué. They hold glue better than regular cottons and crease nicely. As a bonus, most batiks have busy patterns that hide appliqué stitches well.

D VINTAGE FABRICS

Although vintage fabrics have their charm, how you plan to use the finished quilt determines whether you should use them or not. Depending on their age, they are often fragile and just don't hold up under regular washing, so it's not recommended to use them on bed or snuggle quilts. If the end use for a project is a wallhanging or other piece that won't be washed, vintage fabrics have a better chance of holding up over time.

COLLECTING FABRICS

As you start your appliqué journey, you begin to look at fabric differently. You see it not for what it is but for what it can become. Checks on point become pineapples, gradations of the same color become flower petals, and spirals become tree leaves. Train your eye to see the possibilities of each fabric and let this vision help your appliqué come alive.

What Size?

Scraps, fat eighths, and fat quarters are perfect sizes to start a fabric collection. First, save all scraps as you sew. Anything larger than about a 2″ × 2″ square is fair game for appliqué. When purchasing new fabrics for appliqué, you rarely need more than a fat quarter of any one fabric, making it easy to collect a wide variety of fabrics economically.

Style

A **Solids** are great for modern quiltmaking. Simple modern shapes look good in solids and can be used in combination to create bold, graphic appliqué designs. Near-solids and small-scale, dense prints work like solids but add a bit of texture to a design and can be used interchangeably with solids.

B **Black** is not a common choice for traditional appliqué, but it does have its place in modern quiltmaking (see *Cascade*, page 101). For both black solids and black prints, be sure to use smoke-colored invisible thread to hide the stitches.

C **Prints** with graphic elements such as polka dots, squares, stripes, and so on are great choices for modern appliqué. You can use the fabric's pattern on the appliqué shapes to make it look like you did more work than you really did. Busy prints hide invisible stitches very well, making them the perfect fabric to use when beginning appliqué. They also provide a wide variety of texture and color to add interest to appliqué shapes.

Preparing the Fabric

As with gathering the right tools, preparing fabrics properly makes the appliqué experience go more smoothly.

TO PREWASH OR NOT TO PREWASH APPLIQUÉ FABRICS

When piecing, whether to prewash or not is a matter of personal preference. In appliqué, however, you should always prewash. The fabric needs to be clean and free of sizing, starch, or other chemicals, and you should be confident the shapes won't shrink or bleed the first time you wash the quilt.

Advantages of prewashing

Prevents shrinking: All cotton fabric shrinks, but not all fabric shrinks equally. On a pieced quilt, this variable shrinkage can be attractive, adding to a soft, vintage feel. With appliqué, however, if the appliqué shapes shrink more than the background fabric or vice versa, the effect might not be pleasing.

Prevents bleeding: Some fabrics—especially dark, rich colors—bleed. Although fabrics are much better today than they used to be, it still happens. Prewashing reduces the chance of dark fabrics bleeding onto light ones the first time you wash the finished quilt.

Prevents crocking: Crocking is bleeding's ugly stepsister. Those same dark, rich fabrics that bleed in the wash can also rub off onto another fabric even when dry. Crocking can happen on a folded, finished quilt, especially a high-contrast quilt—think red and white. So even if you never plan on washing a quilt, crocking can still cause you grief.

Removes sizing and other chemicals: When preparing appliqué shapes using the standard freezer-paper method, you'll get the best results if the fabric doesn't have the original sizing or other chemicals that are used in the manufacturing process. Sizing, chemicals, and starch can all inhibit the freezer paper from adhering to the fabric, making the process frustrating. Prewashing eliminates this frustration.

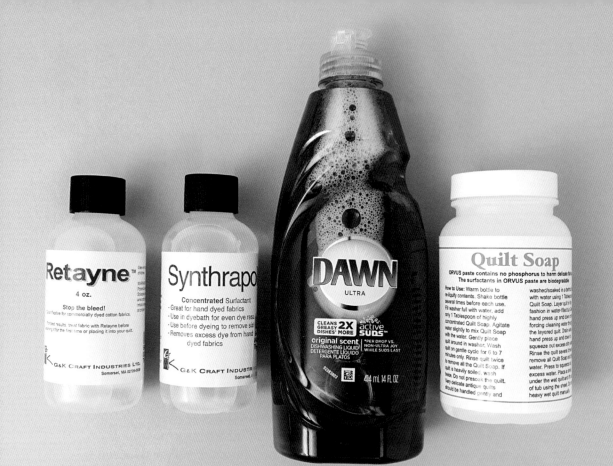

HOW TO WASH FABRIC

Sort yardage into lights and darks, and wash in the machine with the soap or fixative of your choice (see below and page 19). If using a specialty soap, follow the directions on the package. Dry in the dryer with no dryer sheets or other fabric softener, which will interfere with the adhesive on the freezer paper. Remove promptly when dry, and press.

What product should you use?

There are many options for what kind of soap or fixative to use when pre-washing fabric. The following are some of the more popular products and how they are used. Look for them online or at local quilt shops.

Retayne: Retayne sets the dye when you are washing new fabric for the first time. Once washed in it, fabrics won't bleed or crock. You can use it in the washing machine or when washing by hand with hot water. Once you've treated a fabric, you don't have to repeat the process. You can even wash new clothes, such as jeans and blacks, in Retayne to keep them from bleeding and fading. Retayne does not inhibit the fabric from sticking to the freezer paper. I wash all my fabrics in Retayne the first time they are washed.

Synthrapol: This sizing and dye remover is used when hand dyeing fabric to remove excess dyes. It also keeps dyes from redepositing on other fabrics during the wash. The original Dawn dishwashing liquid has a similar chemical mix. I use 1–2 tablespoons of Dawn to wash all my quilts once they are complete. It can also be used to prewash yardage.

Orvus paste soap: Orvus is a gentle soap used to bathe livestock. What makes it great for fabric is that it contains no brighteners, fabric softeners, or fragrances—all of which can damage fabric over time (and all of which are found in everyday laundry detergent). You can buy Orvus in small quantities in quilt shops (under the name Quilt Soap). If you have access to a farm supply store, you can buy it in large quantities, which is much more cost-effective.

Orvus can be used to prewash fabric, but it's not specifically intended to prevent bleeding or crocking. It is a good option for washing finished quilts.

Prewashing vintage fabrics, stash fabrics, or precuts

At some point you will want to appliqué with fabric that isn't newly purchased quilter's cotton. It might be a piece of vintage fabric that you bought online or something dug out of your stash from years ago. You may or may not know the history of such a piece.

The best way to wash these fabrics is by hand, hanging them up to drip dry. It's not as convenient as using the machine, but these older fabrics may be more delicate and need a little tender loving care. If you are really concerned about a piece, wash a 2″ × 2″ square first to see how it reacts to washing. If it washes fine, then proceed with the entire piece. The same goes for precut fabrics such as charm squares and jelly rolls. Wash them by hand to keep them from raveling and balling up in the machine.

BACKGROUND FABRICS

I also recommend prewashing fabrics that will be used for the background for the same reasons mentioned on page 17—shrinking, bleeding, and crocking. Unwashed fabric does have a nice feel and crispness to it, though, so if you don't want to give that up, starch it back to that feel after it's washed.

I find it easiest to wash all my fabrics as soon as I acquire them. That way I don't have to wonder if a piece has been washed, and I don't have to scramble to wash a piece from my stash at the last minute—especially if I decide I want it to be an appliqué shape instead of a background.

Standard Freezer-Paper and Fabric Preparation

Once you have gathered supplies and prepared the fabric, you are ready to prepare the appliqué shapes. The best way to learn is by doing, so the following steps are designed for you to follow along and create your own sample heart appliqué block. Once you have mastered the techniques, you can adapt them to any project.

For the practice block, choose two fabrics—one for the heart and one for the background. Cut a 7″ × 7″ square of the background fabric. Use the heart pattern (below) for the appliqué, and follow the steps.

Practice Heart

Heart pattern for practice block

Prepare the Background Fabric for Appliqué

1. Cut the background. The process of appliquéing can shrink or distort a block, especially if the design involves a lot of pieces per block. To allow for this shrinkage, cut the background about ½″ larger than the finished block size each way. The extra size also helps for squaring up the block after appliquéing.

2. Starch the background. Starch the background blocks to the desired stiffness. You'll get a feel for how much starch you need as you gain experience with the appliqué process. Thicker fabrics might need no starch at all, but most fabrics need some starch so the appliqué stitches don't bunch up or the appliqué shapes don't pucker as they are sewn. In general, the stiffer the background, the better the results in the finished block will be.

I prefer to work with a super-stiff background. Since freezer paper makes the appliqué shapes stiff, having an equally stiff background makes sewing go smoothly. This is completely a matter of personal preference, however. Experiment to see how much starch you prefer for backgrounds.

To make the background super-stiff, douse the fabric in a thick spray of starch until it is soaked. Let it soak in for a minute or two and then, with a dry iron, gently press until dry. Be sure to press gently and with the grain to minimize distortion. I recommend a dry iron because using steam causes white flecks of starch "dandruff" to form. It also causes the iron to stick to the fabric.

3. Press registration marks. Once the block is dry, gently press it in half in both directions to form a plus sign at the center. Depending on how complex the design is, you might also need to press it in half on both diagonals to form an X. These registration marks will aid in the placement of the appliqué shapes later.

4. Mark the seam allowance. Since the background is cut oversized, it's easy to lose track of the parameters of the finished block when placing the appliqué shapes. If you need a visual aid to help you stay within the finished block size, put a small dot on the four corners at the finished size. This will show you the outer boundary of the block as you are placing the shape so you don't accidentally place it in the seam allowance.

Press the registration marks into the background and mark the seam allowance.

Trace the Pattern on Freezer Paper

Cut a piece of freezer paper larger than the pattern and lay it on top of the pattern with the dull side up. Trace the shape using a sharp pencil. Freezer paper is thin enough for you to see most patterns through, but if you need to, use a lightbox or tape it to a window to see the pattern.

Trace the pattern on freezer paper.

Lightbox

If you don't own a lightbox, tape the pattern to a window and trace onto the freezer paper. Another method is to put a lamp underneath a glass-top coffee table and then trace.

Cut Out the Freezer-Paper Templates

1. Using paper scissors, cut out the shape on the drawn line. Take large, smooth cuts by holding the scissors steady and moving the freezer paper. Short snips create jagged edges. When the shape is cut out, turn it over and look from the back side for any jagged edges. Smooth out any you find by carefully recutting.

Keep in mind that the finished appliqué shape will look exactly like the freezer-paper template. If you want the appliqué shapes to be perfect, make the freezer-paper templates perfect.

Cut out the freezer-paper shape on the drawn line.

2. If you need multiple copies of the same shape, trace the shape once and cut 2 more pieces of freezer paper. Stack all 3 freezer-paper pieces with the traced shape on top and staple together in 2 or 3 places, being careful not to staple over the drawn lines. Stapling the pieces keeps them from shifting as you cut out the pattern. A stack of 3 is the right number for cutting—it's hard to accurately cut out more than 3. Once the stack is cut out, remove the staples. Repeat to make the needed number of shapes.

NOTE *For instructions on how to trace and cut more complex and layered patterns, refer to Layered Patterns in Part III: Advanced Preparation Techniques (page 53).*

Press and Cut the Appliqué Shapes

1. Once the freezer-paper template is prepared, place it *shiny side down* on the *back* of the fabric. As a general rule, place curved parts of shapes on the bias when you can. Bias tends to mold to the curved edge of the freezer paper, making perfect results easier. Straight lines can be placed either on the bias or on the straight grain.

With a *hot, dry iron*, press the shapes to the wrong side of the fabric, leaving a minimum of ½″–¾″ between shapes. This leaves enough room for the seam allowance when you cut out the shapes.

Tip
The patterns in this book are *reversed* for this method of machine appliqué. When you iron the freezer-paper template to the wrong side of the fabric, the appliqué shape will appear as a mirror image of the pattern.

2. Cut out the fabric shape with fabric scissors, leaving a scant ¼″ seam allowance beyond the edge of the freezer paper. Keep the seam allowance as consistent as possible and try to avoid jagged edges. On tight curves and sharp points, trim the seam allowance to slightly less than a scant ¼″.

Cut out the shape with a scant ¼″ seam allowance.

For inner curves, snip the seam allowance every ⅛″–¼″ along the curve. Straight edges and outer curves don't need to be clipped. Clipping weakens the fabric, so you want to clip each shape as little as possible but enough to make the inner curve smooth. For deep V's, as in the heart shape, clip straight down, stopping just a few threads before the edge of the freezer paper.

Clip straight down in the V on the heart, stopping just a few threads before the edge of the freezer paper.

NOTE *For more instructions on clipping inner curves and similar shapes, refer to Inner Curves in Tips for Gluing Common Appliqué Shapes (page 32).*

Glue the Seam Allowance

1. Place the fabric shape on a worktable in front of you, on top of a piece of plain paper. With the gluestick, run a line of glue along the seam allowance and the outer edge of the dull side of the freezer paper. Don't skimp on the glue—you need enough glue to make the seam allowance stay down and to be able to reposition if necessary. It will be washed out, so don't worry about stiffness or possible negative long-term effects on the finished quilt.

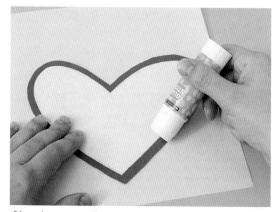

Glue the seam allowance and the edge of the freezer paper with a gluestick.

2. Next, pick up the fabric shape, holding it with the glued side toward you. Beginning on the straightest edge, take small pinches with your finger and thumb to fold the seam allowance over to the dull side of the freezer paper. You can feel the edge of the freezer paper as you fold over the seam allowance— use this as a guide. As you pinch the seam allowance down, be careful not to create puckers and sharp points along the edge. Continue around the shape until you get back to where you started.

Using your fingers, take small pinches to fold the seam allowance over the edge of the freezer paper.

NOTE *Your fingers will get sticky with the glue as you prepare the shapes. Either keep a wet towel handy to wipe the glue off your fingers or wash them frequently as you prepare the fabric shapes.*

3. When you are done, turn the fabric shape over and make sure the edges are smooth and look the way you want them to look. If not, you have a small window of opportunity to make changes before the glue sets. Gently lift up the edge of the seam allowance and redo it. If you have trouble correcting the problem with your fingers, try using a stiletto to work it smooth. If you still can't smooth it, you'll have to decide if you can live with small imperfections or if you need to start over. When you have it as perfect as you want it to be, the shape is finished and ready to be sewn onto the background fabric.

The finished heart shape from the back

The finished heart shape

TIPS FOR GLUING COMMON APPLIQUÉ SHAPES

In appliqué, the same types of shapes come up over and over. There are different ways to prepare each of them. The following are tips for handling various types of shapes.

Points

DULL POINTS

These points range in angle from about 30° to 180°. Dull points are the easiest to create. Simply glue and fold one side of the point, and then glue and fold the other side.

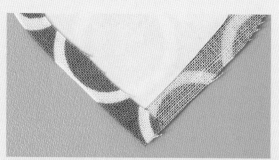

Glue and fold over the first side of the point.

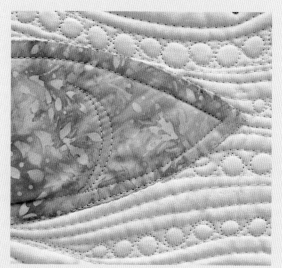

The fish's nose in Fish (page 131) is a dull point.

Glue the second side, making sure to glue on top of the seam allowance from the first fold. Fold over and pinch down the second side of the point.

Turn the shape over and check the point to make sure the seam allowance underneath isn't showing on the front. Correct any problems before the glue dries.

SHARP POINTS

Sharp points are among the hardest shapes to prepare with freezer paper, but with practice even the sharpest points can come out perfectly.

First, fold the point of the fabric seam allowance straight down to the point of the freezer paper (the fold is perpendicular to the axis of the point). Then trim the seam allowance on either side of the point to just under 3/16˝. Be careful not to cut too close to the edge of the freezer paper. Run a line of glue along one side of the point and fold it over. You can just see the outline of the point underneath the fabric—make sure the fold touches the point of the freezer paper. Repeat with the other side. The second side is the important side because it determines whether the point will be sharp.

NOTE *The presser foot on a sewing machine can smash a sharp point when it's being sewn down, distorting and flattening it. To keep this problem to a minimum, walk the stitch slowly by hand, using the hand wheel.*

The extremely sharp points of the geese shapes in Geese (page 107) are attainable with a little practice.

Glue the tip of the fabric point and fold it over, straight onto the point of the freezer paper.

Trim each side of the seam allowance to a scant 3/16˝. You need enough seam allowance to fold over, but not so much that it goes beyond the point and shows from the front.

Glue and fold over one side of the point. Use the edge of the freezer paper as a guide to align the fabric at the point.

Glue the second side of the point and fold it over. This side will determine whether the point is sharp or not, so take care.

Look at the front to see if the point looks the way you want it to look. Make any changes now.

NOTE It's easy for the second fold to poke out on the side, showing on the front of the shape, if the seam allowance isn't cut narrow enough. To fix this issue, carefully fold the seam allowance back under the point, and glue it. This method will add bulk, so you'll have to take special care when sewing and when removing the freezer paper. Avoid trimming the extra seam allowance off with scissors—it's too easy to trim too close to the point and ruin the shape.

Curves

OUTER CURVES

Gentle outer curves are easy to prepare. Fold over the seam allowance and pinch it with your fingers like normal. There is no need to clip the seam allowance—the natural give of the bias will allow the fabric to hug the edge of the freezer paper perfectly.

Outer curves don't need to be clipped.

For a tighter outer curve, such as the end of an oval, trim the seam allowance a little less than a scant ¼˝ and take tiny pinches just along the very edge of the freezer paper. Then, after you have the seam allowance tacked down and you're happy with how smooth it looks from the front, you can go back and finger-press down the rest of the seam allowance.

Cut the seam allowance slightly less than a scant ¼˝.

Take tiny pinches along the edge of the freezer paper. Check the front to see if it's as smooth as you want it. Make any changes now.

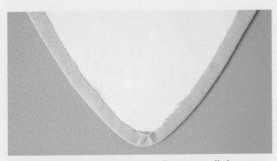

Go back and pinch the seam allowance all the way down.

Double-check the front to make sure it's smooth. Make any changes now before the glue dries.

INNER CURVES

Inner curves need to be clipped before they are glued. Clipping allows the seam allowance to fold over properly without stretching or warping. Using small, sharp scissors, clip straight into the seam allowance, stopping just a few threads before the edge of the freezer paper. Be careful not to snip into the freezer paper, or the cut will show on the front of the shape, leaving a small hole that will fray over time. Clip every ⅛˝–¼˝, or slightly closer together for tighter curves.

After clipping, run a line of glue on the seam allowance and on the edge of the freezer paper. Depending on how many clips you took, you might have to run the gluestick out, perpendicular from the freezer paper, rather than parallel to the edge, so that the clipped parts don't bunch up and fold back on themselves.

Fold the seam allowance over and take small pinches to secure it. Turn the shape over and look at the curve from the front. If the clips are too far apart, the edges between the clips will be straight, not curved, making the curve look jagged. In that case, use a stiletto to manipulate the curve to get it closer to smooth. With experience, you'll get a feel for just how far apart to clip the seam allowance.

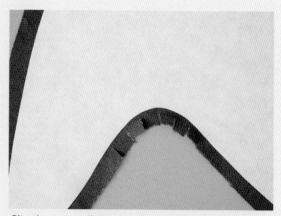

Clip the seam allowance about every ⅛˝–¼˝ along the edge of the inner curve.

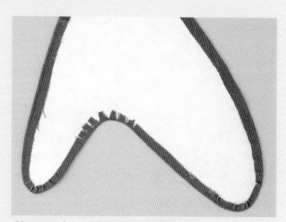

Glue and fold over the seam allowance.

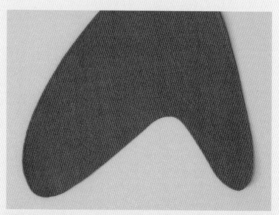

Check the front of the shape to see if it's as smooth as you want it. Make any changes now, before the glue dries.

Deep V Shapes

A deep V—as in a heart shape—usually needs just one clip straight into the V, ending just a few threads before the freezer paper. If it's a super-deep V, cut the seam allowance larger than ¼˝, to as much as ½˝. You'll need the extra seam allowance to have something to glue down to the freezer paper.

The tree in Trees (page 93) has a deep V.

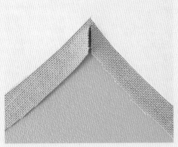

Cut out the shape with a scant ¼˝ seam allowance. Clip straight down into the V to just a few threads before the edge of the freezer paper.

Glue and fold over the seam allowance.

Turn the shape over to make sure the V is completely covered and no raw edge of the seam allowance shows from the front. If necessary, make changes now, before the glue sets.

Small Shapes

Small shapes can test your patience, especially when you feel like your fingers are too big to handle them! The best way to prepare the smallest of shapes is to use a stiletto to help hold the shape flat on the table in front of you while turning the seam allowance under with either your finger or another stiletto.

Oversized Shapes

Oversized shapes need special handling during preparation. They tend to warp as you glue around them, making the seam allowance uneven by the time you get back to the starting point. To minimize this natural tendency, lay the large shape flat on a table and work around the perimeter, handling it as little as possible. Use a stiletto rather than your fingers to fold the seam allowance over. If the shape lies flat after preparation, it will lie flat after it is appliquéd on the block.

Place the Shapes on the Background Fabric

1. Once the shapes are prepared, it's time to glue them to the background block. Refer to the pattern placement guide that accompanies most appliqué projects (some guides are on the pullout for this book) or the photo of the finished block to see where to place them. On only the seam allowance, dot white glue from the needle-nose applicator bottle around the edge of the shape. Use the smallest amount of glue necessary to hold the shape in place until it is sewn, usually only about 6–8 dots per shape. Place the glued shape on the background, making sure it's not in the seam allowance of the background block, and gently press it down with your fingers.

2. If you need to reposition the shape, gently pull it up, reglue it, and reposition it. Since you used a small amount of glue, the shape can come off easily to correct a mistake even if the glue has dried.

Dot tiny drops of glue on the seam allowance around the perimeter of the shape.

Place the shape on the background and press it down with your fingers.

The Stitching Process

Sewing with invisible thread is much like sewing with regular thread, but there are some extra considerations to take into account.

Set Up the Sewing Machine

1. Wind the bobbin. Wind the bobbin with invisible thread *slowly* and fill the bobbin only half full. Invisible thread will stretch and constrict on the bobbin. Winding at the normal speed only accentuates that tendency. If your machine uses plastic bobbins, this constriction will make it hard, if not impossible, to get the bobbin off the winder.

If you have trouble getting the end of the thread to catch and wind properly, start with a long lead of thread and wind it by hand to start it. Then use the machine's pedal to wind it the rest of the way. Starting by hand should give you enough of a head start that the thread will catch and wind properly until the bobbin is half full. Remember, if you struggle with winding the invisible thread on the bobbin, try a different brand of thread. Some machines work better with one brand than with another.

2. Thread the machine. Thread the machine as usual. The invisible thread actually goes through the needle more easily than regular thread, but sometimes it's hard to see it happening. I find that more light helps. A gooseneck lamp placed behind the machine with the light shining directly behind the needle makes it easier to see the thread and needle. You can also mark the tip of the thread with a black marker to help you see it as you guide it through the needle.

3. Set up the zigzag stitch. Although you can use any stitch or combination of stitches to sew the shapes, I find a narrow zigzag is the best starting point. It is a sturdy stitch that will hold the shapes securely, and it disappears when used with the invisible thread.

Experiment with the width and length of the zigzag to see what works for you. The exact width and length are largely personal preference, depending on what looks good to you. Start out with a rather wide stitch until you get the hang of stitching around curves without going off the shape. As you get better, you can reduce the width to as narrow as you can manage, just wide enough so the stitches hold the shape down and disappear into the fabric. Once you have the stitch width and length decided, you're ready to start sewing.

This is the stitch width and length that works best for me. I set my Bernina 930 to a no. 2 (2mm) stitch length and width. Test several settings on your machine before you decide what is best for you.

Sew the Shapes

In the following examples, I used a high-contrast thread to show the process of attaching the appliqué so you can really see what to do. You'll use invisible thread for your sample block.

1. Start stitching on the straightest side of the shape, not at a point or corner. Leave a long tail, about 3″, when starting. Stitch around the shape, being careful to keep the stitches mostly on the appliqué shape with just the point of the zigzag going into the background fabric.

Leaving a long tail, start sewing the shape using the zigzag stitch.

2. At first go slow, especially on the curves. It's very easy to sew off the shape if you go too fast. As you get better, you can increase the speed.

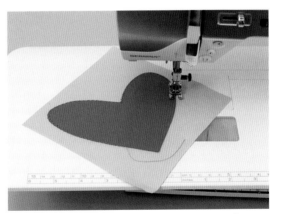

Continue sewing around the shape, keeping the stitch on the shape with just the point of the zigzag going into the background fabric.

Tip

When appliquéing shapes that have a bulky seam allowance, like those with sharp points, it might be necessary to walk the stitches by hand with the hand wheel through the thick sections. Resume stitching with the foot pedal once you clear the trouble spots.

3. About halfway around the shape—or as soon as you can lift the block comfortably to see your starting point from the back—stop sewing with the needle down, lift the block, and pull the top thread to the back. Trim both threads, leaving about a 1″ tail. This will help make the stopping point easier to finish off after you sew back around to the starting point.

To pull the top thread to the back, gently rock the bobbin thread back and forth until the top thread pops up. Grab that loop with your fingers and pull to the back and trim. This keeps the front of the appliqué block feeling smooth to the touch. Sometimes that top thread just doesn't want to pull through to the back side. In these cases, just leave it as is and cut the thread off flush with the line of stitching on the front after you're done sewing the shape down. Since you will backstitch at the end, it will stay tight and won't unravel.

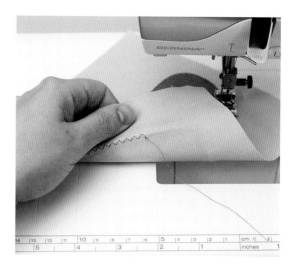

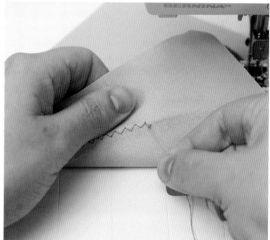

About halfway around the shape, lift the block and pull the top thread to the back of the block. Trim both the threads, leaving about a 1″ tail.

4. Continue sewing around the shape after pulling the top thread to the back. When you get back to the starting point, sew over the beginning stitches by about 3 or 4 stitches and then backstitch 1 or 2 stitches. You don't want to backstitch too much, or it will show on the quilt top. Just a few stitches are enough to keep the shape secure. Clip the threads, leaving them long, and remove the block from the machine. Pull the top thread to the back as you did before, and trim both threads to about 1″.

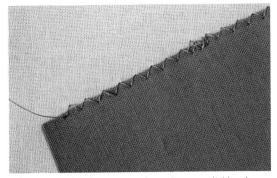

When using high-contrast thread on a solid background and the zigzag stitch, you can really see the stopping point. If you want a high-contrast look, choose a stitch that hides the starts and stops well.

When using the zigzag stitch with invisible thread, you can barely see the stopping point.

Tip: Plan Ahead

The most time-consuming part of sewing the appliqué is the starts and stops. To make the sewing process go faster, evaluate the block before you start sewing and plan a path that will allow for the fewest starts and stops. For simple shapes, this path is easy to determine, but for more complex and layered patterns, use your finger to trace possible paths over all the shapes until you determine the best path. Starts and stops are inevitable, but minimizing them will make the stitching go faster and more easily.

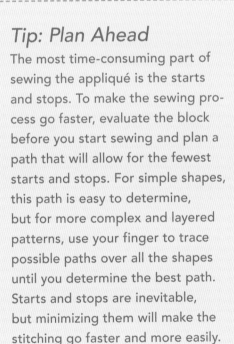

Complete the Appliqué Block

1. Cut out the background. Once the shapes are sewn, the freezer paper needs to come out. Using a small, sharp pair of scissors, from the back carefully cut out the background fabric, leaving ¼˝ around the inside of the appliqué shape. The freezer paper will act as a barrier between the background fabric and the appliqué fabric, but you still need to take care not to poke the scissors through to the front of the freezer paper and risk snipping a hole into the appliqué shape on the front.

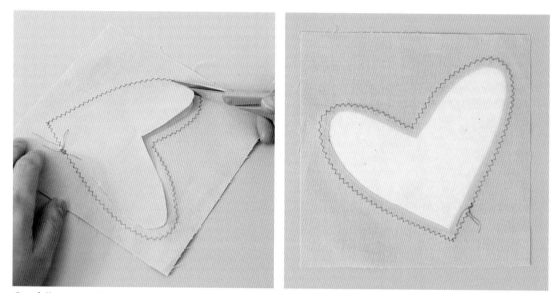

Carefully cut out the backing with small, sharp scissors. Keep the seam allowance even and smooth.

2. Remove the freezer paper. After the backing is cut out, take the block to the sink and hold it under the water to dampen the glued edges of the appliqué. Turn it over to get the front wet as well. Place the block flat on a terry cloth towel and roll it up to squeeze out the excess water. You can also use a spritz bottle filled with water to dampen the block.

Let the block sit in the towel for a few minutes to soften the glue so the freezer paper will slip out easily. Gently pull the block in both directions on the bias until the freezer paper starts to pull away from the stitches. The stitches act like perforations and help the paper come out easily. Use your fingers to gently pull the paper the rest of the way out of the block.

If the freezer paper doesn't come out easily, rewet, let it sit longer, and try again. It should come out the second time. Usually not soaking the block enough or not letting it sit long enough after soaking are the two main reasons the freezer paper doesn't come out easily the first time.

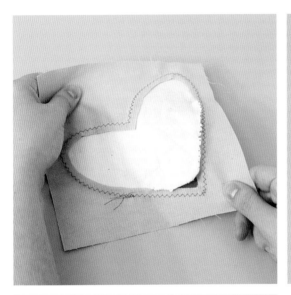

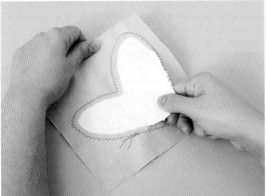

Pull the block gently on the bias in each direction to get the freezer paper to come apart from the stitching. Once it's loosened, use your fingers to pull out the freezer paper.

Sometimes the freezer paper doesn't come out in one piece, and little bits are left behind in the stitching—especially in the tips of points. Use tweezers to pick out the last bits. Be careful not to grab the stitches and pull them instead of the freezer paper. Sometimes it's okay to leave in a small amount of stubborn freezer paper that just won't come out, so don't stress over getting every last bit. You just want the bulk of it out so the block isn't stiff or crinkly when complete.

Use tweezers to gently pick out the larger bits of freezer paper that were left behind.

3. Finish the block. Once all the freezer paper is out of the appliqué shapes, hang the block on a pants hanger and let it drip dry. If you are in a hurry, you can press the block dry, but be careful not to stretch it as you press.

When the block is dry, press it and trim it to the correct size. The block is now complete and ready to be sewn into the quilt top.

NOTE *Sometimes the appliqué appears to be wrinkled and have puckers along the edge even after the block is dried and pressed. A few wrinkles are okay—they will quilt out flat.*

The finished block, ready to be sewn into a quilt top.

The finished block sewn with invisible thread.

PART II: Alternatives to Invisible Zigzag Appliqué

Once the shapes are prepared, you can appliqué them to the background fabric in any way you choose. I prefer the look and feel of invisible thread for most applications, but there are many times in modern quiltmaking when you might want to use other threads or stitches to get a different look.

When branching out from invisible thread, there's a lot to think about. Different threads and stitches yield different outcomes. Understanding what you want the end result to be will help you choose.

Thread to match the appliqué shapes and a near-invisible stitch will allow the appliqué to stand out. Contrasting thread and a bold stitch will become part of the overall design, giving it a contemporary feel. Or maybe the look you want is a combination of both—you don't have to use the same stitch and thread throughout one block. Think it through ahead of time and audition the options before deciding.

For modern quilters, endless combinations of stitches coupled with a wide array of threads open up more design options than could ever be completed in one lifetime. And with the modern sensibility, what once was the standard now doesn't have to be the *only* way to do it. The limitations are merely time and imagination!

Thread

Thread is the most important tool in your sewing supplies. It's inexpensive and plentiful. Thread companies work hard year after year to develop more and more styles to keep us sewing.

The study of thread could keep you busy for hours, but to get started, there are just a few things you need to know. Other than color, thread comes in different weights (thicknesses) and finishes that you will need to take into consideration when determining how you want the appliqué to look.

Weight: The weight of the thread comes into play when determining whether you want it to show or be hidden on the appliqué. In general, the larger the weight number, the thinner the thread, so a higher weight will disappear more on the appliqué, and a lower one will show more. Most quilters use 50 weight for machine piecing, and it also works well for almost all appliqué. In addition, try 40 weight and 60 weight to see if they make a noticeable difference for the project.

Finish: The finish is how the thread looks—is it dull (matte) or shiny (with a sheen)? Some silk and rayon have a high sheen, cotton has a matte finish with no sheen, and polyester is somewhere in between.

Cotton: Cotton thread is the most common choice for all of quiltmaking. It's a natural fiber, which appeals to many quilters. It comes in virtually any color, and it's inexpensive. Almost any appliqué stitch a machine has will look good with cotton thread, and you probably have enough of a variety of colors in your stash to get you started. Overall, cotton is the best option.

Polyester: Like cotton, polyester thread comes in a wide array of colors and is inexpensive. Polyester thread has less lint than cotton. It's stronger than cotton and colorfast. It has a touch of sheen, which is nice in the finished appliqué. I use it interchangeably with cotton threads.

Rayon: Rayon thread has a high sheen, making it perfect when you want the appliqué stitch to be the star, such as with a satin stitch. It's comparable to silk thread but much less expensive. It comes in a wide variety of colors and is available everywhere.

Variegated: Sometimes you might want the look of a variegated thread, especially if the appliqué shapes are colorful. Matching the thread to the colors in the shapes softens the look of the thread and accentuates the appliqué shape. Variegated threads come in cotton, polyester, and rayon.

Silk: Silk is a strong natural fiber. It comes in a variety of sheens to match various needs. It is very beautiful in the finished appliqué and glides easily through the needle. However, it is more expensive than cotton and polyester, and oftentimes harder to find locally.

Different threads give different looks and feels to the finished appliqué. Experiment with cotton, polyester, rayon, variegated and silk threads in a variety of weights to find the look that's best for the block.

Stitches

Just as different threads yield different looks, so do different stitches. The following are just a few of the common options. Most can be executed with only a straight and zigzag stitch. Depending on your machine, you can experiment with other stitches not mentioned here to come up with your own unique style.

The following samples are sewn in contrasting thread so you can see the stitches. Remember that different colors and weights of threads will produce different looks.

Blind Hem Stitch

If your goal is to mimic hand appliqué, as an alternative to the zigzag stitch, the blind hem stitch is a good choice. It takes just the smallest bite into the edge of the shape as you are sewing, so it barely shows. Use a thinner thread (60 weight) in a color to match the appliqué shape or invisible thread to get the full effect.

To sew, set the stitch to a short length and a narrow width—the narrower it is, the less it will show. Sew around the shape until you get back to the starting point. Sew over the starting point by a few stitches and then backstitch. Pull the threads to the back and trim, or trim the threads flush with the top.

Blind hem stitch

Single Straight-Line Stitch

A straight-line stitch is largely used as a utilitarian stitch—used just to get the shape sewn down regardless of the design. It goes fast and is simple. Use it with any thread color that looks good on the shape.

To sew, outline the shape, getting as close to the edge as possible without going into the background. Sew over the starting point by a few stitches and then backstitch. Pull the threads to the back and trim, or trim the threads flush with the top. If you have a top-stitch foot for your machine, it will help keep the stitch even along the edge.

Straight-line stitch

Triple Straight-Line Stitch

For a fun, casual variation, stitch around the shape three times. The first time around, get as close to the edge as possible. The second and third times around, the stitch can vary and even go off into the background a little, depending on the look you want. Finish it as you did for the single straight-line stitch.

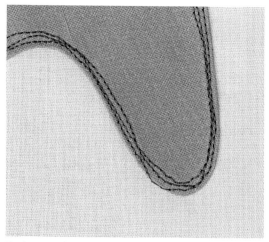

Triple straight-line stitch

Zigzag Stitch

Another utility stitch—the zigzag—should be the go-to stitch for most applications. It has a little flair to add texture and interest, but it's not so overpowering that it takes over and becomes the star of the show. On busy prints and solids alike, it almost disappears when done in matching thread. On solids in contrasting threads, it gives just the right amount of flash. Experiment with oversized widths or long lengths for different effects.

To sew, start stitching on the side of the shape, not a point or corner. Sew around the entire shape, overlap the starting point by a few stitches, and backstitch. Pull the threads to the back and trim, or trim the threads flush with the top.

Zigzag stitch on a print

Scribble Stitch

The scribble stitch is a playful, casual stitch. It's created by setting the machine to a zigzag, sewing a few stitches, backstitching a few stitches over the stitches just sewn, resuming stitching, backstitching again, and so on. Vary how long you stitch before you backstitch each time and move the block as you are backstitching so the backstitch is offset from the forward stitch. Sew around the entire shape, overlap the starting point by a few stitches, and backstitch. Pull the threads to the back and trim, or trim the threads flush with the top.

You can get a similar look by zigzagging around the shape twice, offsetting the stitches the second time, rather than backstitching as you go. It gives a slightly different look, but with the same feel.

Scribble stitch

Blanket Stitch

An old traditional standby—the blanket stitch—has been around for a long time. It's found on new and antique quilts alike and was especially popular in the 1930s. It's most commonly done in black thread no matter what color the appliqué shapes are, which can overpower the shapes, especially if they are on the small side and you use a dense stitch (short length and narrow stitch setting). It is definitely an impressive, show-stopping stitch.

To sew, start stitching on the side of the shape, not a point or corner. Sew around the entire shape until you get back to the starting point. Lock off the stitch, pull the threads to the back, and trim, or trim the threads flush with the top.

Take care at the starts and stops so they blend seamlessly into one another. Some newer machines can compensate to line up the starts and stops with the push of a button. With older machines, more finessing will be needed.

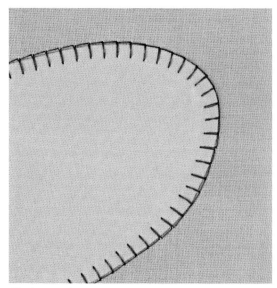
Blanket stitch

Feather Stitch

A feather stitch gives the edge of the shape a spiky look, which can accent everything from rose stems (think thorns) to a fantasy shape from your imagination. The sewing is similar to the blanket stitch—you'll have to take care at the starts and stops to get it to line up. Sew around the entire shape, overlap the starting point by a few stitches, and backstitch. Pull the threads to the back and trim, or trim the threads flush with the top. Once you get the hang of it, the sewing goes smoothly. Experiment with the width and length of the stitch to get widely varying results.

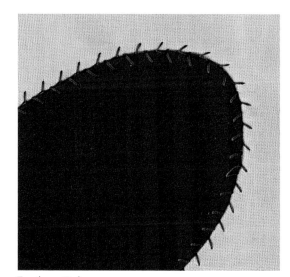
Feather stitch

Decorative Stitches

If you own a machine that has a variety of programmed stitches, you can have a lot of fun experimenting. And don't just limit yourself to traditional quilter's stitches—look at the other stitches too. There might be some unexpected surprises you can use in the right circumstances. You can combine stitches for unexpected results, too—either formal or casual.

The Modern Appliqué Workbook

PART III: Advanced Preparation Techniques

As your appliqué skills improve, you'll want to branch out into more complex shapes and patterns. Here are some of the more common advanced techniques you will encounter.

Layered Patterns

Layered patterns are those that have two or more shapes stacked on top of each other. Layered appliqué shapes need special attention so the freezer paper can be easily removed.

When approaching a layered pattern, follow the instructions given in Standard Freezer-Paper and Fabric Preparation (page 21). The difference will be in the tracing and gluing. Rather than tracing each individual element of the pattern separately, trace the entire pattern as a whole onto the dull side of the freezer paper. Cut out the shapes on the line, being careful to keep track of the parts so you can reassemble them after the shapes are prepared.

Trace the bird pattern (page 83) onto freezer paper and carefully cut out on the lines.

Next, prepare the fabric shapes as usual, pressing the freezer-paper shapes to the back side of the fabric and cutting out the fabric shapes with their seam allowances, but leave the edges unglued on the side of the shape that will be tucked underneath another shape. In the example shown, the body of the bird has a wing-shaped hole in it. The seam allowance of this body edge will lie beneath the actual wing appliqué. In this area, don't turn the body seam allowance under for gluing; just let it stay flat, underneath the wing. When gluing the prepared shapes together, take care to glue the shapes together just on the seam allowance—and don't add unnecessary bulk by overlapping the freezer-paper layers. Once sewn, cut out the background as usual and take out the freezer paper. Since none of the freezer paper overlaps in the sewn block, it should be easy to remove.

Prepare the shapes as usual, but don't turn under and glue the seam allowance on the bottommost part where the wing will attach to it.

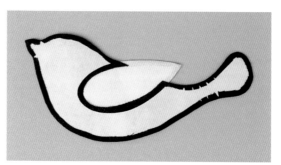

From the back, you can see how the shapes fit together.

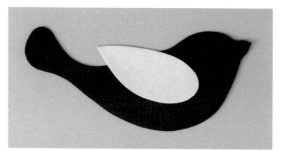

The finished shape is ready to be sewn as usual. When it is time to remove the freezer paper, since none of it overlaps another piece of freezer paper, it will all come out easily without cutting out several layers.

Tip

Typically you want to work from the bottom up when building layered appliqué shapes. That means the bottommost piece will have the unfinished seam allowance so the piece on top of it has something to be glued to. But evaluate each pattern before gluing to determine the best seams to leave unfinished. Sometimes it depends on which shapes are easier to glue or which ones would be easier to leave unglued. At first you may have to try more than one way to see how it looks.

Reverse Appliqué

Reverse appliqué is used when the pieces on a layered shape would be too small or too awkward to prepare with freezer paper, or you just want a different look to the appliqué.

A pattern that is an appropriate candidate for reverse appliqué is one that has an opening or hole in it, such as the pattern from *Baskets* (page 75). To prepare, trace the entire shape on freezer paper and cut it out on the line. Then carefully cut out the opening in the shape on the line, making sure the inside edges are smooth. Press the freezer-paper shape to the back side of the fabric, and cut out and glue as usual. Cut out the center of the handle, leaving about a ¼˝ seam allowance. Clip the inner curves and glue.

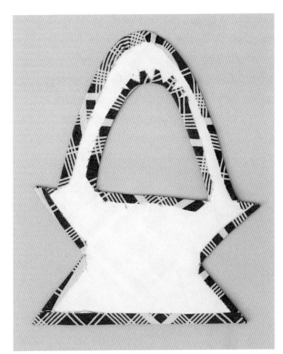

The back side of the prepared basket

The front side of the prepared basket

Once the shape is prepared, determine how big a piece of fabric is needed to fill the opening in the handle. Dot glue around the seam allowance on the back side of the main shape and press it onto the fabric. Check to make sure the opening is filled completely. Trim if necessary so the fabric doesn't show along the outside edges when viewed from the front. Glue the entire unit to the background and sew as usual.

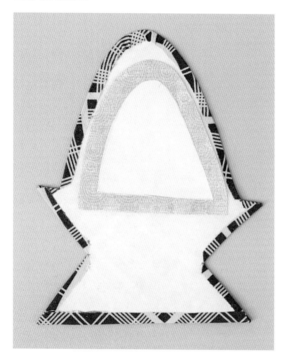

Add the plain fabric to the back of the basket handle opening, making sure it fills the hole completely.

Reverse appliqué in the completed quilt

Reversing the Pattern

Most appliqué patterns are either symmetrical or asymmetrical (directional). A symmetrical pattern looks the same from the back side as it does from the front—it is balanced. A heart, a circle, and a melon shape are symmetrical. So is the pattern for *Star Bright* (page 119).

An asymmetrical pattern is directional—the back is the reverse or mirror image of the front. The bird in *Birds* (page 81) and the flames in *Flame* (page 87) are asymmetrical. In this case, the finished appliqué will be the opposite of the pattern unless you reverse the pattern before cutting your fabric.

When creating shapes using standard freezer-paper preparation, the pattern will automatically come out reversed because the freezer-paper shape is ironed to the back side of the fabric. This is okay for symmetrical shapes, but for directional shapes, you will need to reverse the image when preparing the freezer paper so the shapes will match the pattern when the block is complete.

If you need just one shape reversed, trace the shape onto the dull size of the freezer paper as usual. Cut another piece of freezer paper and staple it, shiny side to shiny side, with the traced piece. Cut out on the line. Discard the traced piece and use the bottom shape for the pattern.

If you need several copies of a shape, some reversed and some not (such as the three birds in *Birds*, page 81), trace one of the shapes as usual on the dull side of the freezer paper. Then cut out two more pieces of freezer paper. Stack them dull side up, but turn over one of the pieces of freezer paper so the shiny side is up. Staple the stack together with the traced piece on top. Stapling keeps the freezer paper from slipping as it's cut out. Cut it out on the line and remove the staples. You will have three identical shapes, but one will be the reverse of the other two.

NOTE *Some patterns reverse the templates for you. Read the pattern to see if it has been reversed. If it has, then you don't need to do anything but trace the pattern on the freezer paper and continue as usual. If it hasn't, you'll need to reverse the patterns. All the directional patterns for the projects in this book have been reversed.*

Precise Placement

I usually prefer a more casual look to my appliqué and find that just eyeballing placement is sufficient. But if you are working on an intricate or symmetrical pattern where precise placement is important, you'll want to take a few extra steps to ensure the pattern is glued perfectly.

First, lay out the full-size pattern on a work surface in front of you and place the prepared shapes on top of the pattern. Then, starting with the bottom layer, glue the shapes to each other. As you glue each layer, lay it back down on the pattern to make sure the shapes match up with the pattern. Once all the shapes are glued to each other and dry, carefully move the appliqué unit to the prepared background fabric and glue it down.

Pieced Appliqué Shapes

Some projects call for the appliqué shape to be pieced before it's prepared for appliqué. In this case, after piecing, *press the seams open* before beginning the freezer-paper preparation process. The seam allowances on the pieced shape will be trickier to glue down, so the less bulk, the better. Pressing the seams open creates less bulk than pressing them to one side. After the pieced shape is ready, continue with the freezer-paper preparation process. When gluing down the seam allowance, look closely to make sure it lies flat and looks good from the front. You might need a bit more glue under the seam allowances to get the shape to lie flat.

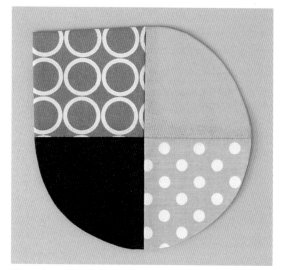

Pieced appliqué shape front

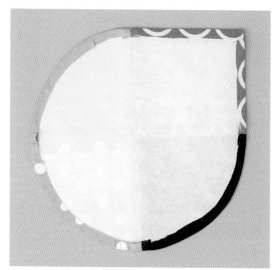

Pieced appliqué shape back

Appliqué on a Pieced Block

Sometimes combining appliqué with a pieced block creates just the look you want, as with the basket blocks in *Baskets* (page 75). But it's easy for the seam allowance on the back to get caught and flip up when appliquéing. This can cause extra bulk and lumps that show up on the front. To combat this tendency, first press the pieced block well, making sure the seams are all neatly pressed open or to one side. Then, when appliquéing the shapes, pay close attention as you go so the seams don't get caught underneath and flip up.

If you have a block with a lot of seams or one made of a fabric that doesn't hold a crease well, use a tear-away stabilizer on the back of the block. Appliqué the block as normal and tear the stabilizer away before cutting out the background to remove the freezer paper.

Bias and Straight- or Cross-Grain Tape

Similar to binding, bias, straight-grain, and cross-grain tape make great decorative elements in appliqué—think flower stems, stained-glass appliqué, and Celtic designs. For modern quilting, bias and straight-grain tape can open up a big world of graphic options.

Tape differs from binding in the way it's made. Rather than folding and pressing the strips in half lengthwise, wrong sides together, as for binding, tape is made with a single fold, by folding both long edges of the strip in to meet in the center. This process turns under both edges, leaving no raw edges exposed.

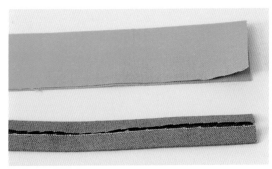

Binding (top) and bias tape (bottom)

Bias Tape

Bias tape is made from strips cut on the diagonal, or a 45° angle, of the fabric. This gives the fabric the maximum stretch and is useful for stems, circles, and other curved shapes. To cut strips on the bias, cut a square of fabric and fold it in half on the diagonal. Line up a ruler on the folded edge and cut perpendicular from the fold to the point of the fabric. Then cut the strips the proper width for the size you need.

A 10″ square yields about 2 yards total of ½″ bias tape.

Straight-Grain Tape

Straight-grain tape is made from strips cut on the length of the fabric. It is used for straight strips that don't need to curve. You can use bias tape for straight stems, but it takes less fabric and is easier to make straight-grain tape. To cut straight-grain strips, cut the fabric as normal on the straight of grain (*length* of the fabric).

Cross-Grain Tape

Cross-grain tape is made from strips cut on the width of fabric (selvage to selvage). The cross grain has a little more stretch than the straight grain, but not as much as bias. Cross-grain tape can be used interchangeably with straight-grain tape. To cut cross-grain strips, cut the fabric as normal on the cross grain (*width* of the fabric).

MAKING BIAS AND STRAIGHT-GRAIN TAPE

There are many methods for making bias tape. I prefer using a bias tape maker, which makes creating bias tape easy and consistent. You can use any method you are comfortable with.

First, determine whether you need bias or straight-grain tape, and then cut the strips to the desired width. The usual formula for the cut width for single-fold tape is to double the finished width, but I find that cutting the strips ⅛″ less than double the finished width works better for me for single-fold tape. Experiment to see what you prefer.

- For ¼″ single-fold tape, cut ⅜″ strips.

- For ⅜″ single-fold tape, cut ⅝″ strips.

- For ½″ single-fold tape, cut ⅞″ strips.

Once you determine the width you need, cut the strips. The projects requiring bias or straight-grain tape in this book will tell you how many total inches you need and how much for each block. Add about 1″ to the length of each strip for tucking under shapes. Make the tape using any method you choose.

If you are working with a pattern where accurate placement is crucial, lay the block on top of the pattern and trace the line of the tape lightly with a pencil. Use that line as the guide and glue the tape down with small dots of glue. Make sure you glue the center of the strip down. Then proceed with the other appliqué shapes on the block.

When using bias tape on a particularly curvy design, use a hot, dry iron to "train" the tape. Lay an end of the tape at the start of the drawn line. Gently press the tape as you continue laying it on the line. You'll see that the tape loosely holds its shape, making it easier to glue and sew down on the line.

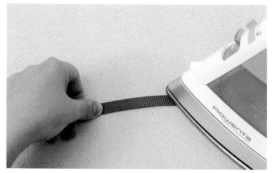

To train the tape to curve, hold the tape with your nonironing hand. Gently stretch and force the curve, pressing as you go.

A piece of bias tape that has been trained. It will hold this shape and be easier to glue to the background fabric.

If the pattern is more casual, you can determine placement as you go. For most patterns you will have a great deal of leeway with placement, so always experiment to see if you can come up with something you like better than what the pattern indicates.

Usually the tape will start and stop underneath an appliqué shape, or it will run off the block and be finished off in the seam allowance. If the ends of the tape are not hidden in one of these ways, you'll need to turn them under and glue them down before gluing the tape strip to the block. To do this, open up the tip of the tape and run a small line of glue along the raw edge with a gluestick. Refold the ends back and pinch them shut. Then add a second line of glue along this edge and fold it over to the back, making sure the seam allowance doesn't show from the front.

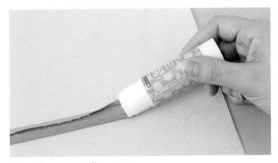
Glue the seam allowance.

Pinch shut.

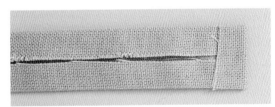
Folded under and glued, back

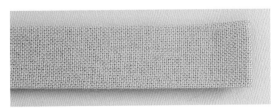
Folded under and glued, front

Use the same guidelines to determine what stitch to use when sewing down the tape as you do for any other appliqué—do you want the stitches to show or be invisible? Do you want the stitching to be the star or just be there to hold it down? Do you want it to be formal or casual in feel? The stitch you use for the tape doesn't have to be the same stitch you use on the rest of the shapes in the block. Mixing and matching stitches can create visual interest for the block.

Modifying a Commercial Pattern

One of the least-used options quiltmakers have in their toolbox is redrawing an appliqué pattern to make it easier to accommodate their skill level. If a pattern you would like to make has points too sharp, V's too deep, or circles too small, more times than not you can modify the pattern to make it work without detracting from the original look. Redraw sharp points to make them dull, deep V's to make them shallow, and circles to make them larger—or eliminate some altogether. Evaluate the pattern to see how you can make it work, and do it without guilt.

NOTE *Keep in mind that if you modify a commercial pattern, that does not make it your design. It still belongs to the designer, along with the copyright, and the designer needs to be credited no matter how many changes you make to it.*

Quilting

When quilting an appliqué quilt, there are some things to consider that are different from a pieced quilt. As usual, most of these options are a matter of personal preference.

In general, there are three options for quilting an appliqué quilt:

- **Custom quilting on the appliqué shape:** This is an option to consider for several reasons. The first is overall durability. Heavy quilting makes any quilt—pieced or appliqué—last longer. If the appliqué quilt will be used daily and washed often, quilting on top of the appliqué will help it hold up better over time.

  Similarly, the size of the appliqué shapes is important to take into consideration. The oversized shapes of the circles and ovals in *Mod* (page 69) are too large to go unquilted. The quilt wouldn't hang properly on the wall or it wouldn't hold up under washing if used as a throw without some quilting holding the shape down.

  Another consideration is how the quilt will look. Quilting on the shapes adds another level of complexity and interest—texture in general is more interesting than a flat surface. It can also further define the shape. If the appliqué is a tree, leaves quilted in the canopy make the context understood—the shape is a tree. Feathers on a bird, spirals on curly hair, or gills on a fish can help define the shapes. This double defining of a shape adds a subtle second level of understanding to the work.

Leaves quilted on a tree in Trees *(page 93) add texture and context to the shape.*

No quilting on the appliqué shape: This is a good option when the appliqué is the star of the quilt and you don't want anything to detract from it. This might be because the appliqué is attached with a decorative stitch or contrasting thread that needs to stand out on a busy print, and you don't want the quilting to overshadow or disappear into the shape.

Something else to consider: Leaving shapes unquilted will let them stand out from the quilt, giving it a look of trapunto, or a three-dimensional quality. This effect is more noticeable if you quilt tight around the shape, allowing it to pop up. This works especially well for small shapes that don't need to be quilted for durability.

Quilting with an allover quilting design: Typically quilting an appliqué quilt with an allover design diminishes the effect of the appliqué. You've worked hard to create the quilt top—you don't want to weaken its impact with quilting that detracts from that work. Imagine how a Baltimore Album quilt would look with an allover design—the quilting would diminish all the hard work and minimize the beauty of the appliqué.

That being said, modern quilts have more freedom with the "rules." In some cases where the appliqué shapes are bold and graphic, an allover design can work, especially when it's well thought out and part of the overall visual effect of the quilt.

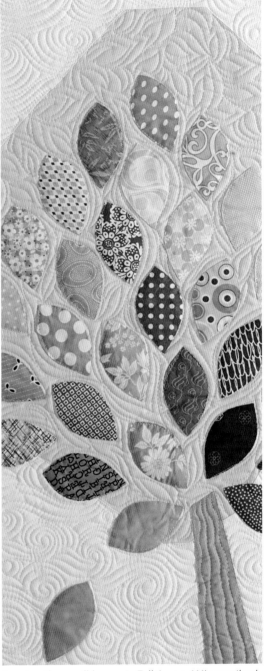

Leaving the small leaves in Fall (page 111) unquilted adds a three-dimensional look to the quilt.

Binding

After quilting, square up and trim the excess batting and backing even with the edge of the quilt top.

Often, binding is thought of at the last minute or not thought about at all, other than for its functional qualities, but binding offers one last chance to add to the quilt's design. It can be an active part of the design. It can be a frame for the quilt. It can disappear off the edge of the quilt, leaving the center to be the star.

Several projects in this book have a specific style of binding that somehow enhances the overall design of the quilt. *Birds* (page 81) uses a flange to add a bit of needed color to its edge; *Geese* (page 107) uses a wider binding to stand out and boldly frame the quilt; and the binding on *Flame* (page 87) matches the background of the quilt so it doesn't detract from the design. Each of these projects has instructions to make these bindings.

Unless noted, the binding strips are cut crosswise at 2½˝ wide. If needed for length, join the strips with a diagonal seam. Fold the binding in half lengthwise, press, and use your favorite method to sew it to the quilt.

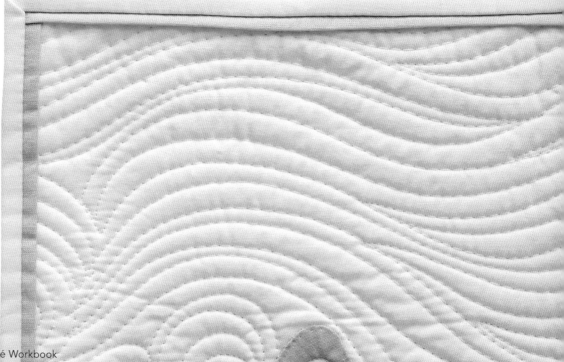

PART V: The Projects

The quilts in this book are designed to be easy and quick to finish so you can get started successfully on your appliqué journey. Each project lists the new appliqué methods used and where to find them in the book so you can easily refer back as you make the quilt. Choose your favorite, gather your tools, and get started!

A ¼˝ seam allowance is used for the projects unless otherwise noted. The usable width of fabric is 42˝.

See the pattern pullout for large patterns. Smaller patterns are included with the projects in the text.

MOD

QUILT: 40″ × 40″ • BLOCK: 18″ × 18″

Design note: If the 60s color combination isn't your thing, try a four-step gradation of a single color with a dark in the center and a light for the largest circle.

Methods: Standard Freezer-Paper and Fabric Preparation (page 21), Oversized Shapes (page 33), Layered Patterns (page 53), The Stitching Process (page 35)

FABRICS

MOD: made by Jenifer Dick, quilted by Angela Walters

APPLIQUÉ:
- 1 fat quarter (18″ × 21″) blue solid

⅝ YARD EACH:
- Brown solid
- Orange solid
- Olive green solid
- Gold solid

BACKGROUND AND BORDERS:
- 1½ yards light gray (fabric 1)

BACKING:
- 1⅝ yards light gray or medium print

BATTING:
- 45″ × 45″

BINDING:
- ½ yard light gray (fabric 2)

APPLIQUÉ SUPPLIES:
- See Tools and Supplies (page 8).

Background

From the light gray (fabric 1), cut 4 strips 2½˝ × width of fabric. Set them aside for the border.

Cut the remaining light gray into 4 squares 19˝ × 19˝. Starch each square with the desired amount of starch.

Appliqué

Using the patterns (see pattern pullout page P1) and the quilt photo for color placement, prepare 4 sets of circles/ovals using the standard freezer-paper method.

To make the templates, trace the entire set of shapes onto an 18˝ piece of freezer paper. Cut out the outer circle carefully on the line. For the inner ovals, cut straight in from the edge of the outer circle to the line of the largest oval. Then cut the oval out on the line. Repeat with the remaining 2 ovals. Repeat with 3 more pieces of freezer paper to make 4 sets of templates for each shape.

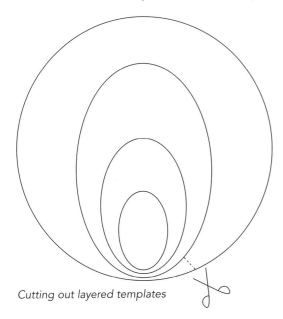

Cutting out layered templates

Cut the fabric shapes and glue the appropriate seam allowances under. Keep in mind that oversized appliqué shapes can become distorted as you glue, causing the seam allowance to be off by the time you get back to the starting point. To alleviate this tendency, lay the shape flat on a large surface as you glue the seam allowance and use a stiletto to fold over the seam allowance (rather than your fingers). This will keep the large shapes flat and easier to appliqué. Note that the curved seam allowance around the inside edge of the outer circle is not turned under—it lies flat because the largest oval is placed on top of it. Similarly, the inner curve of the largest oval lies flat, as does the inner curve of the middle oval.

Once the shapes are prepared, glue them together, stacked on top of each other. They should nest together perfectly. Center and glue the stacks on the prepared background blocks. Appliqué each shape with invisible thread and a zigzag stitch. Remove the freezer paper and press.

Trim the blocks to 18½˝ × 18½˝.

Assembly

Determine the placement of the 4 blocks and make a large four-patch block by sewing 2 sets of 2 blocks together. Press the seam allowances in opposite directions, and then join the rows. Press. Measure vertically through the middle of the quilt top and cut 2 border strips this length. Sew to the sides of the quilt top. Press the seam allowances toward the border. Repeat with the top and bottom borders.

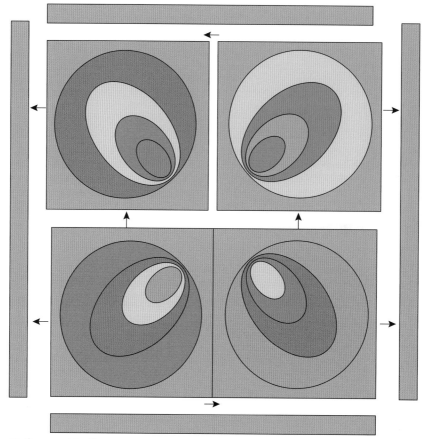

Quilt assembly diagram

Backing

Piece the backing to 45″ × 45″.

Layer and baste the quilt sandwich (page 63).

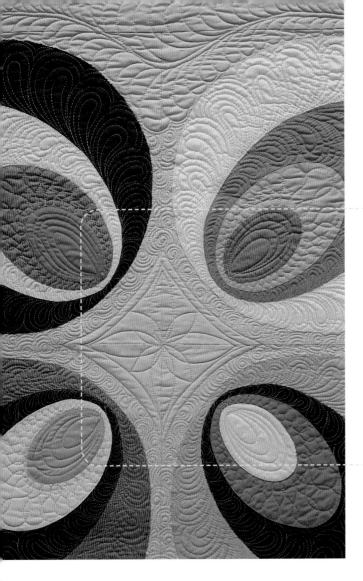

Quilting

Mod is a great quilt top in which to use a variety of fills to add texture to its large open, solid spaces. A quilted medallion in the center is an unexpected visual surprise, and the fills on the ovals and circles are consistent throughout. Feathers along the four edges complete the quilting.

Binding

Prepare 180″ of light gray (fabric 2) binding, and bind using your favorite method. Binding in a slightly darker shade of gray adds a subtle frame to the quilt, stopping the action of the quilting.

BASKETS

QUILT: 18″ × 18″ • BLOCK: 9″ × 9″

Design note: Although I like the quirkiness of placing the blocks in all different directions, *Baskets* could easily be made with the blocks all standing upright. Or you could sew the four blocks all in a single row for a different look.

Methods: Standard Freezer-Paper and Fabric Preparation (page 21), Reverse Appliqué (page 55), Appliqué on a Pieced Block (page 58), Zigzag Stitch (page 49) with contrasting thread

FABRICS

BASKETS: made by Jenifer Dick, quilted by Angela Walters

APPLIQUÉ:

- Scrap (minimum 11″ × 13″) of green plaid for baskets
- Scraps (3″ × 3″) of 3 green prints and 1 orange print for basket centers

BLOCKS:

Starch each block fabric with the desired amount of starch.

- 5″ × 5″ squares of 3 orange prints and 1 green print
- Scraps (minimum 10″ × 10″) of 2 blues—1 print and 1 solid—for backgrounds
- Fat quarter (18″ × 21″) cream (makes 2 backgrounds)

BINDING:

- ⅜ yard blue print

BACKING:

- 23″ × 23″ blue print or cream solid

BATTING:

- 23″ × 23″

APPLIQUÉ SUPPLIES:

- See Tools and Supplies (page 8).

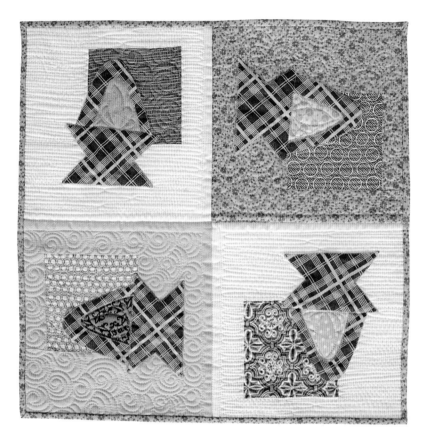

Blocks

From each background fabric,* cut:

    1 strip 1½˝ × 5˝

    1 strip 2˝ × 6˝

    1 strip 3½˝ × 6˝

    1 strip 4˝ × 9½˝

* Cut 2 strips of each size from the cream fabric.

Pair the green 5˝ × 5˝ square with the blue solid strips, 2 orange squares with the 2 cream strip sets, and the remaining orange square with the blue print strips. Referring to the diagram, lay out the pieces for each block and sew together, starting with the top strip, then the 2 sides, and finally the bottom strip. The arrows show the pressing direction.

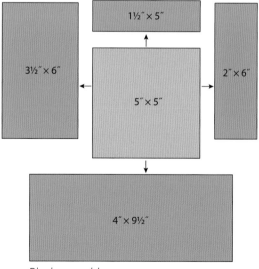

Block assembly

Make 4 blocks 9½˝ × 9½˝, 2 cream and 2 blue.

Appliqué

Using the pattern (below), prepare 4 baskets from the plaid fabric, using the standard freezer-paper method and reverse appliqué for each basket handle. Make a basket with an orange center and 3 baskets with a green center.

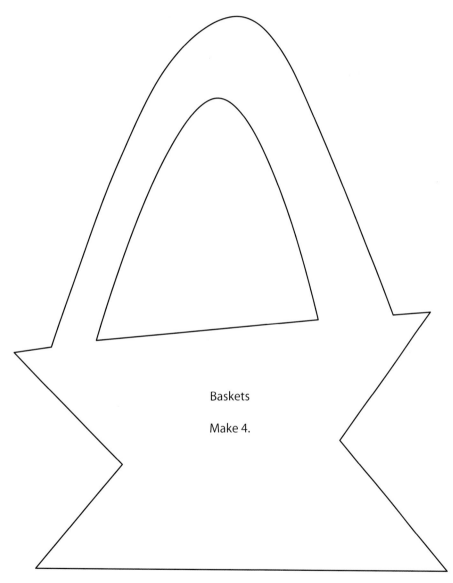

Baskets

Make 4.

Lay out the 4 prepared background blocks all facing the same direction (with the long strip along the bottom). Glue the basket with the orange center on the blue solid block with the green center. Glue the remaining 3 baskets on the remaining blocks. Each should be off-center slightly.

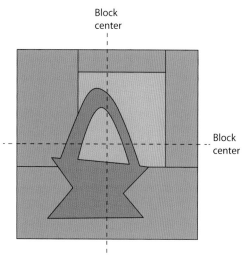

Appliqué placement diagram

Appliqué each shape with contrasting thread and a narrow zigzag stitch. Remove the freezer paper and press.

Assembly

The quilt top is assembled like a four-patch block. Determine how you want the blocks to be configured and sew pairs together in 2 rows. Press the seam allowances in opposite directions. Join the rows and press. The arrows show pressing direction.

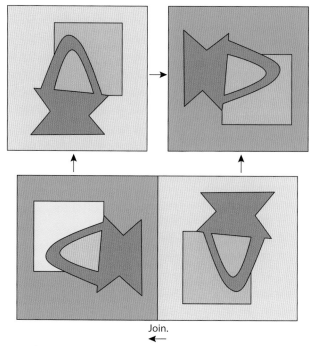

Quilt assembly diagram

Quilting

Layer and baste the quilt sandwich (page 63).

Alternating quilting swirls and stripes fill each block—swirls on the blue and stripes on the white. The small square in each block is the opposite—swirls in the cream and stripes in the white. The baskets are unquilted, but a small motif fills the space inside the handle.

Binding

Prepare 87″ of blue print binding, and bind using your favorite method.

BIRDS

QUILT: 16˝ × 20˝

Design note: These charming birds can be stacked as close or as far apart as you like. Just make sure the spacing in between is consistent.

Methods: Standard Freezer-Paper and Fabric Preparation (page 21), Press Registration Marks (page 22), Layered Patterns (page 53), Reversing the Pattern (page 56), The Stitching Process (page 35)

FABRICS

APPLIQUÉ:
- Scraps (minimum 6˝ × 9˝) of 3 pinks—light, medium, and dark

BACKGROUND:
- 1 fat quarter (18˝ × 21˝) white

BACKING:
- 21˝ × 25˝ white

BATTING:
- 21˝ × 25˝

BINDING:
- ⅜ yard white or pale pink for binding
- ⅛ yard pink for flange, if desired

APPLIQUÉ SUPPLIES:
- See Tools and Supplies (page 8).

BIRDS: made by Jenifer Dick, quilted by Angela Walters

Background

Starch the white background fabric with the desired amount of starch.

Press in half both vertically and horizontally to create registration marks.

Appliqué

Using the pattern (at right), prepare 3 birds using each of the 3 pinks for the body and a wing. Combine the shapes in any way you choose. Be sure to reverse a bird. Once all the shapes are prepared, glue a wing to the body of each bird. Note that the seam allowance of the body where it surrounds the wing is unglued. The wing is glued to this seam allowance.

Glue the middle bird on the center of the background using the pressed registration marks to center it. Then glue the remaining 2 birds—the first above and the second below the centered bird. Be sure to space the 3 birds equally.

Appliqué each bird using invisible thread and a zigzag stitch. Remove the freezer paper and press.

Trim the background to 16½″ × 20½″.

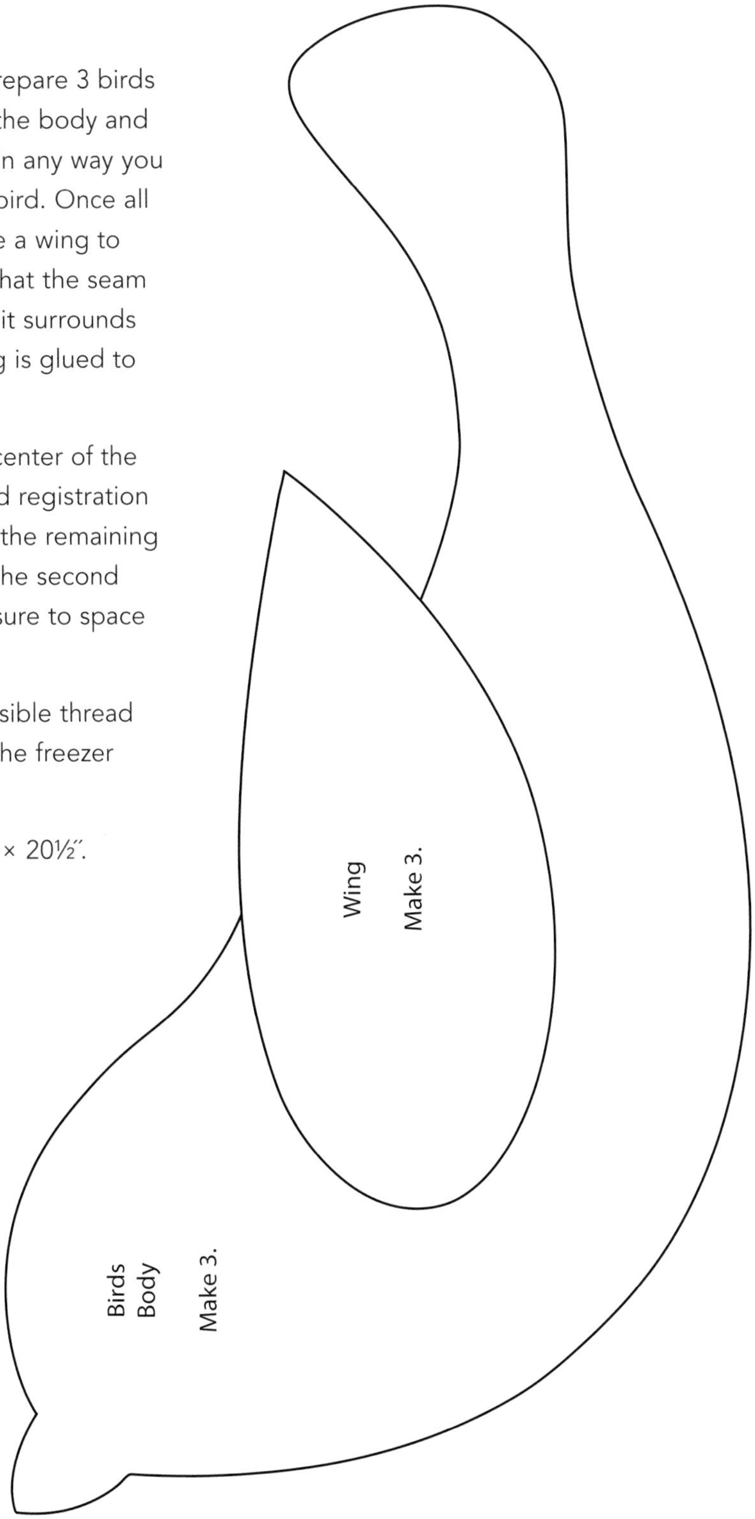

Wing

Make 3.

Birds Body

Make 3.

Quilting

Layer and baste the quilt sandwich (page 63).

Dense quilting of wavy lines and swirls creates the illusion of a gentle breeze to keep the birds aloft. The birds themselves are too large to leave unquilted, so each body and wing is sparsely quilted.

Binding

Binding not only finishes the edges, but it also stops the action of the design. In this case, a white-on-white edge, which I originally was planning, didn't add enough definition to stop the overall visual effect of the design. I could have made the binding with one of the pink fabrics used for the birds, but I decided that would be too heavy for this delicate quilt. What it needed was a small bit of color—a flange—added to the white binding.

A flange is just a small strip of fabric inserted underneath the binding. It sticks out just enough to add a little bit of color but not enough to overpower the design.

To make a flange, cut 1˝ strips of the desired color. For *Birds*, you'll need about 80˝ total, or 2 strips cut from the width of the fabric. Join the strips on the diagonal and press in half lengthwise. Measure the edges of the quilt and cut the strips to those lengths.

Pin the flange to each side of the quilt so the fold is on the inside, overlapping the strips at the corners. Baste in place using a seam allowance less than ¼˝ and a long stitch. Once the flange is basted, bind the quilt as normal with about 90˝ of prepared white binding.

FLAME

QUILT: 17″ × 41½″

Design note: There are so many solids available now that collecting the nine-step gradation from deep red to yellow is fun! When I'm collecting fabrics for a quilt, I cut 2″ swatches to take to quilt shops so I know what I have and what I still need. For this quilt, I found that a 2″ swatch wasn't enough—I took the entire fat quarter with me! The gradations are so subtle that you need a large piece of each fabric to compare to make sure they will blend seamlessly.

Methods: Standard Freezer-Paper and Fabric Preparation (page 21), Inner Curves (page 32), Sharp Points (page 29), Layered Patterns (page 53), Appliqué on a Pieced Block (page 58), The Stitching Process (page 35)

FABRICS

FLAME: made by Jenifer Dick, quilted by Angela Walters

APPLIQUÉ:

- Scraps of 9 solid gradations from deep red to yellow. Label the fabrics 1–9, starting with the deepest red as fabric 1 and the yellow as fabric 9.

Color	Scrap size
1	6″ × 8″
2	6″ × 6″
3	8″ × 12″
4	6″ × 6″
5	8″ × 12″
6	6″ × 6″
7	8″ × 12″
8	6″ × 6″
9	8″ × 14″

BACKGROUND AND BINDING:

Starch each background fabric with the desired amount of starch.

- ½ yard cream solid
- ½ yard blue-green

BACKING:

- 22″ × 47″ cream solid

BATTING:

- 22″ × 47″

APPLIQUÉ SUPPLIES:

- See Tools and Supplies (page 8).

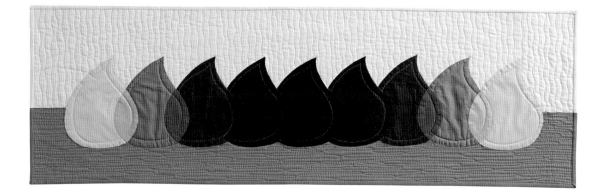

Background

From the cream, cut 1 strip 10˝ × width of fabric.

From the blue-green, cut 1 strip 8˝ × width of fabric.

Sew the 2 background strips together on the long edges and press toward the blue-green side.

Appliqué

Each flame is made of the main body and the melon shapes that overlap on each side to create the transparency effect. The center flame will be the deepest red, gradating out to yellow on both ends.

Using the patterns (page 89), prepare 2 main-body flame shapes from each of fabrics 3, 5, and 7 and 1 main-body flame shape from fabric 1. Then from fabric 9, prepare 1 main-body shape that includes the left-side melon and 1 main-body shape that includes the right-side melon. Finally, prepare 2 melon shapes from each of fabrics 2, 4, 6, and 8. When preparing the main-body shapes, be sure to leave the edges along the 2 sides unglued (the parts that go underneath the melon shapes). This will give you something to attach the melon shapes to and help line them up when you glue them together. Refer to the diagram for color placement for each unit. Note that the color gradation is the same on both sides, moving outward from the center flame.

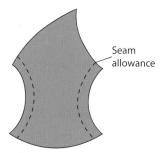

Seam allowance

When preparing the main body of the flames, leave the seam allowance on each side unglued.

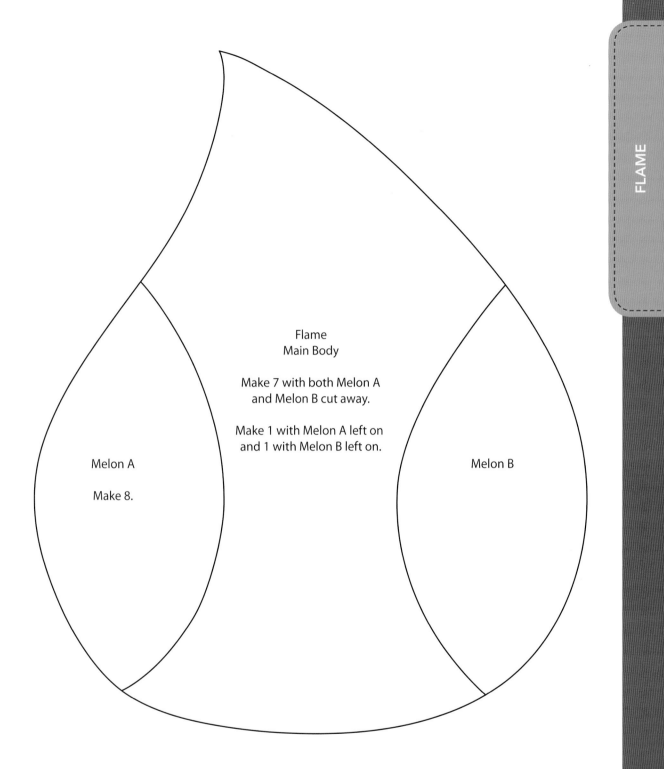

Flame
Main Body

Make 7 with both Melon A
and Melon B cut away.

Make 1 with Melon A left on
and 1 with Melon B left on.

Melon A

Make 8.

Melon B

To assemble the flames, lay out the 9 main-body shapes in a straight row roughly where they will be when finished. Lay the melon shapes between each pair of main-body shapes. Now is the last time to check that each color flows into the next one without any color standing out. Make any changes now if the flow doesn't work.

Dot glue around the backs of the melons in the seam allowances. Place melon shapes on the seam allowances of the main body, starting in the center and working out. Pay close attention to the top and bottom points of each melon shape—the points where the melons meet the main body should be perfectly aligned to get the illusion to work. You have time before the glue dries to make any changes as you go through this process.

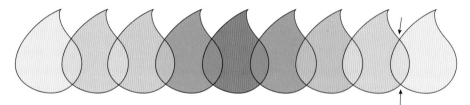

To get the transparency effect to work, make sure the points of the melon shapes line up at the intersections where the main bodies of the flames meet.

Once all the shapes are glued together and dry, move them to the prepared background. Place the unit wherever you like on the background. It can sit on top of the blue-green strip or lower, as shown in the quilt photo. Glue it in place and appliqué each shape with invisible thread and a zigzag stitch. Remove the freezer paper and press.

Quilting

Layer and baste the quilt sandwich (page 63).

Squiggly vertical lines in the white background imitate heat rising from the flames. Continuous horizontal lines in the blue give it a vague feeling of water—a nice contrast to the heat of the flames. The flames themselves are sparsely quilted—just enough to hold them down—letting the transparency effect of the flames be the star.

Binding

The two-color background of the quilt poses a binding challenge. Do you bind it in the cream, which would be awkward in the blue section of the quilt, or do you bind in the blue, which would pose the same problem in the cream section? I chose to make a two-color binding, which gives the illusion that the quilt is not bound at all—the background just stops.

To make the binding, cut 2 binding strips the width of the fabric from both the cream and the blue. Trim the selvage edges and sew the cream strips to the blue strips on the short straight edge (not on the diagonal, which is the norm), and press the seams open. Press each strip in half lengthwise. Each strip will be about 80˝ long.

Pin a binding strip to one side of the quilt top where the cream and blue meet. Make sure to double-check that the binding and the quilt top align perfectly. Pin the rest of the binding on, allowing for the turn at the corners. At the top and the bottom of the quilt, leave a long tail. Sew on the binding. Repeat with the second strip on the other side of the quilt. Join the binding at the top and bottom.

TREES

QUILT: 41″ × 49″

Design note: I found a striped green fabric that happened to have all the greens, browns, and creams I wanted. If you are unable to find a green stripe that suits you, you can piece your own panel with a variety of greens, browns, tans, and creams in a mixture of solids and prints. Add in a blue-green or another unusual color for interest.

Methods: Standard Freezer-Paper and Fabric Preparation (page 21), Layered Patterns (page 53), The Stitching Process (page 35)

FABRICS

TREES: made by Jenifer Dick, quilted by Angela Walters

APPLIQUÉ:
- Scraps (from 3″ square to 15″ square) of up to 7 *each* different greens and browns in a mixture of solids and prints

BACKGROUND:
- 1⅛ yard cream
- ¾ yard green stripe (if stripes run the length of the fabric) or ⅞ yard green stripe (if stripes run across the width of the fabric)

BINDING:
- ½ yard light tan or cream

BACKING:
- 2½ yards cream

BATTING:
- 46″ × 54″

APPLIQUÉ SUPPLIES:
- See Tools and Supplies (page 8).

Background

From the cream, cut:

> 1 strip 20˝ × width of fabric. Trim the selvage off a side. Starch this cream background strip with the desired amount of starch.
>
> 1 strip 5½˝ × 30½˝
>
> 1 strip 11½˝ × 30½˝

From the green stripe, cut 1 panel 24½˝ × 30½˝, making sure the stripe is horizontal (parallel to the 24½˝ dimension).

Appliqué

Using the patterns (pages 96 and 97 and pattern pullout page P1), prepare 7 tree tops and 7 tree trunks. Be sure to spread out the green and brown values so they aren't all bunched up together. Glue the tree trunks to the matching tops.

On the cream background fabric, make a light pencil mark in the seam allowance 5¼˝ and 29¼˝ from the cut edge (the right-hand edge of the background). The space between the marks should measure 24˝.

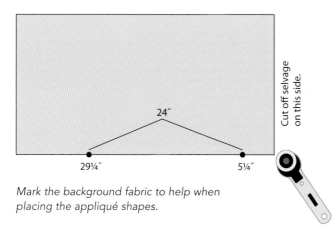

Mark the background fabric to help when placing the appliqué shapes.

Referring to the quilt photo for placement, glue the prepared trees on the cream background fabric between the marks. Make sure the bottoms of the trunks hang off the bottom edge by about ¼˝. You want them to catch in the seam allowance of the background. Appliqué each shape with invisible thread and a zigzag stitch. Remove the freezer paper and press.

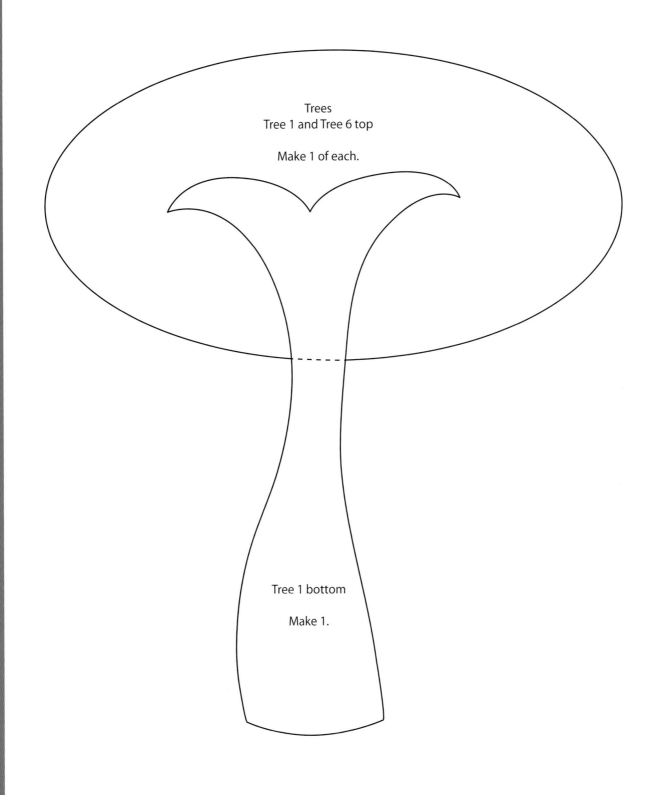

Trees
Tree 1 and Tree 6 top

Make 1 of each.

Tree 1 bottom

Make 1.

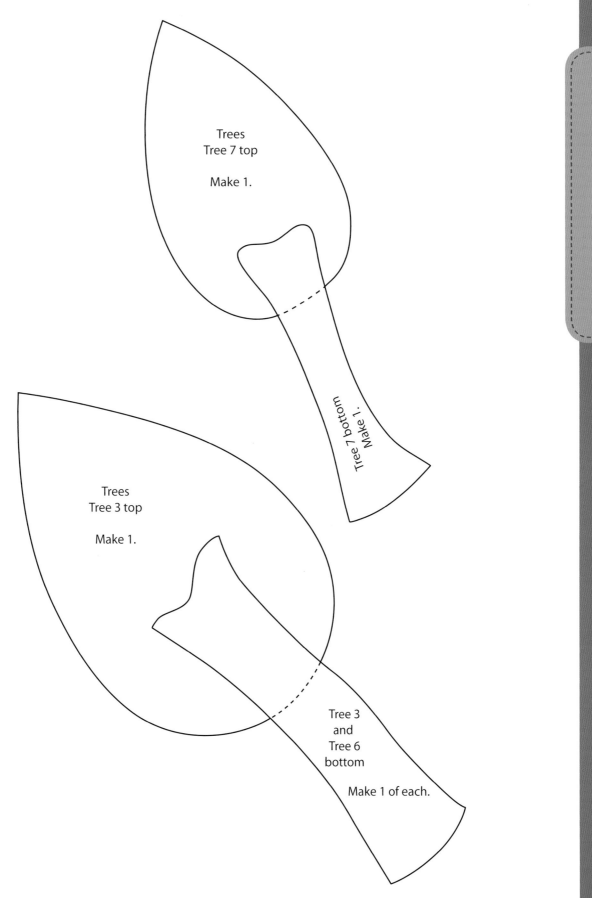

Trees
Tree 7 top

Make 1.

Tree 7 bottom
Make 1.

Trees
Tree 3 top

Make 1.

Tree 3
and
Tree 6
bottom

Make 1 of each.

Assembly

Referring to the quilt assembly diagram, sew the 5½˝ cream strip to the right-hand side of the green striped panel and the 11½˝ cream rectangle to the left. Sew this joined rectangle to the top appliqué panel, matching up the marks on the panel with the green striped panel. The arrows show the pressing direction.

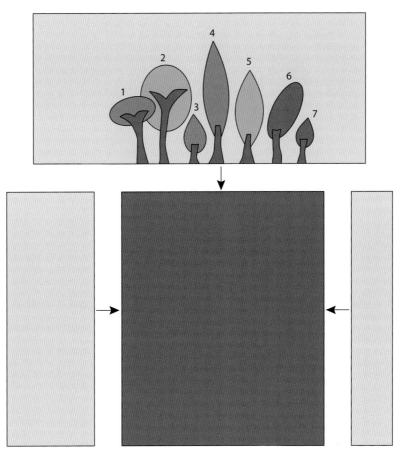

Quilt assembly diagram

Backing

Piece the backing to 46˝ × 54˝.

Layer and baste the quilt sandwich (page 63).

Quilting

A variety of textures fill
the background—from
swirls around the trees
to squiggles and larger
swirls below. The trees
are heavily quilted with a
variety of leaf shapes, and
each trunk is outlined.

Binding

Prepare 200″ of light tan
or cream binding, and
bind using your favorite
method.

CASCADE

QUILT: 27½″ × 30½″

Design note: Any color will make the grays pop, so choose your favorite color if you like something else better than chartreuse.

Methods: Standard Freezer-Paper and Fabric Preparation (page 21), Press Registration Marks (page 22), Triple Straight-Line Stitch (page 48) with matching thread

FABRICS

CASCADE: made by Jenifer Dick, quilted by Angela Walters

APPLIQUÉ:
- Scraps (8″ × 8″) of 5 gradated solids: light gray, medium-light gray, medium gray, medium-dark gray, and black

BACKGROUND:
- 1 fat quarter (18″ × 22″) chartreuse
- ⅞ yard white

BACKING:
- 1 yard white

BATTING:
- 33″ × 36″

BINDING:
- ⅜ yard black

APPLIQUÉ SUPPLIES:
- See Tools and Supplies (page 8).
- Thread to match each gray

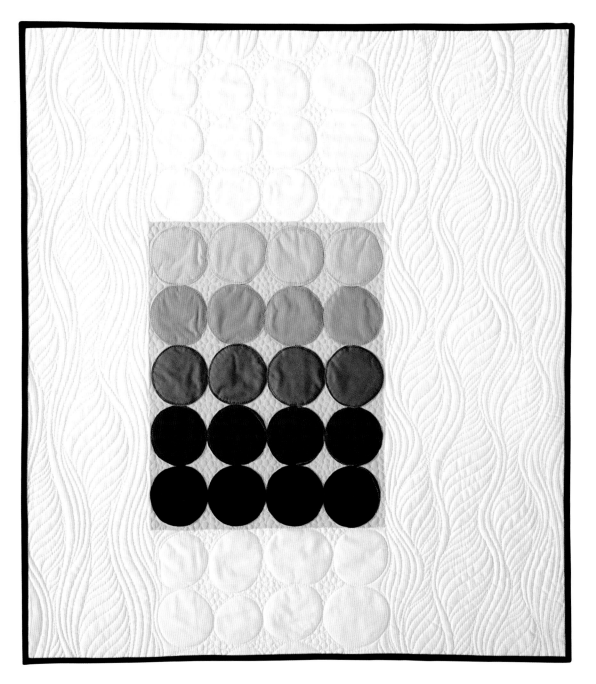

Background

Cut the chartreuse fabric into a 13″ × 16″ rectangle. Starch to the desired
stiffness, fold in half, and press in both directions to make registration marks.

Appliqué

Using the pattern (below), prepare 4 circles 3″ diameter of *each* color for a total of 20 appliqué circles, using the standard freezer-paper method.

Tip

If you find tracing a perfect circle is difficult, use a compass. Instead of tracing the pattern by hand, set the compass to draw a 3″-diameter circle and draw the circles on the freezer paper. This is a bit faster and makes more accurate circles than tracing.

Finger-press the 4 medium-gray circles in half. Match up the creases on the circles with the horizontal pressed line on the background. The edges of the circles should just touch each other. Glue each down using the fewest drops needed to hold each circle in place. The vertical pressed line on the background should fall exactly between the 2 center medium-gray circles.

Fill in with the rest of the circles, making sure the vertical pressed line is exactly in the center of the 2 middle columns and each circle touches its neighbor both horizontally and vertically. Make sure none of the circles extend beyond the 12″ × 15″ finished size of the chartreuse center panel.

Appliqué the shapes using a straight stitch and thread to match each shape. Circle around each shape 3 times, being sure to catch as close to the edge as possible at least once without going into the background. Remove the freezer paper and press the panel.

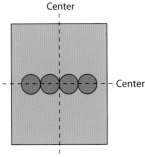

Circle placement diagram

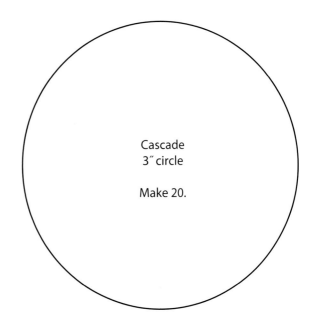

Cascade
3″ circle

Make 20.

Assembly

Trim the appliqué panel to 12½″ × 15½″.

Borders

From the white background fabric, cut:

    1 strip 7″ × 15½″

    1 strip 7″ × 28″

    1 strip 9½″ × 15½″

    1 strip 9½″ × 28″

Sew the 7″ × 15½″ strip to the left side of the panel and the 9½″ × 15½″ strip to the right side of the panel. Take care when sewing that you don't catch the edges of the circles in the seam allowances. Press the seam allowances toward the panel.

Finish the quilt top by sewing the 7″ × 28″ strip to the top of the panel and the 9½″ × 28″ strip to the bottom. Press the seam allowances toward the panel.

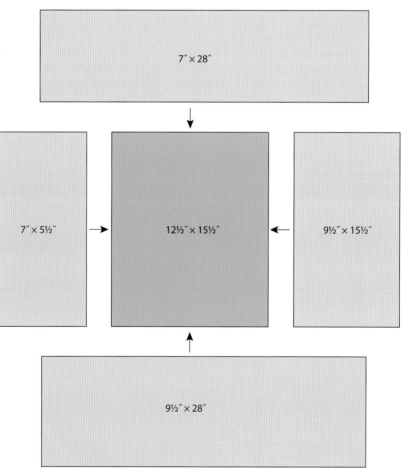

Quilt assembly diagram

Quilting

Layer and baste the quilt sandwich (page 63).

Quilted circles above and below the panel continue the illusion of the appliqué circles floating off the quilt. Tiny circles fill in behind both the appliqué circles and the quilted circles, making them pop out. The sides are serpentine ropes running the length of the quilt, adding vertical movement.

Binding

Prepare 136˝ of black binding, and bind using your favorite method.

Black binding, although not common, works for *Cascade*. The black next to the white background is not too harsh because the black is a repetition of a color already introduced in the center of the quilt. But most of all, it is an elegant way to finish the quilt.

GEESE

QUILT: Approximately 44½″ × 29″

Design note: Sometimes using all solids can go flat—especially shades of gray. To make this quilt top come alive, throw in a print or two to mix things up. Also, remember that creative quilting can add visual interest to the finished quilt. (See Quilting, page 64, for more on the quilting.)

Methods: Standard Freezer-Paper and Fabric Preparation (page 21), Sharp Points (page 29), Single Straight-Line Stitch (page 48)

FABRICS

GEESE: made by Jenifer Dick, quilted by Angela Walters

APPLIQUÉ:

- 1 fat quarter (18″ × 21″) *each* orange solid and dark gray solid
- 9″ × 11″ scrap *each* gold solid and gold print

BACKGROUND:

- ⅔ yard light gray solid
- ½ yard medium gray solid
- ½ yard light yellow solid

BACKING:

- 1½ yards light yellow

BATTING:

- 35″ × 50″

BINDING:

- ½ yard black solid

APPLIQUÉ SUPPLIES:

- See Tools and Supplies (page 8).

Background

From the light gray, cut 1 panel 19½˝ × width of fabric.

From the medium gray, cut 1 panel 16½˝ × width of fabric.

From the light yellow, cut 1 panel 13½˝ × width of fabric.

Starch the background fabrics with the desired amount of starch.

Appliqué

Using the 3 patterns (see pattern pullout page P2), prepare an orange geese shape (pattern 1), a gold and a gold print geese shape (pattern 2), and 3 dark gray geese shapes (pattern 3), using the standard freezer-paper method.

Referring to the quilt photo, glue each geese shape in place on its corresponding panel. The orange shape goes on the medium gray panel, the dark gray shapes on the light yellow panel, and the gold shapes on the light gray panel.

Placement of the geese shapes is very casual—position them where you like on each panel. Just make sure to keep the shapes out of the seam allowances. Remember that the panels are cut oversized and will be trimmed after the appliqué is done.

Appliqué the shapes using a straight stitch and rayon thread to match each shape. Stitch as close to the edge of each geese shape as possible when appliquéing. Remove the freezer paper and press the panel.

Assembly

Trim the panels to the following sizes:

Light gray: 18½˝ × 30˝

Medium gray: 15½˝ × 30˝

Light yellow: 12½˝ × 30˝

Join the 3 panels together with the yellow panel in the center. Press the seam allowances after sewing.

Binding

Prepare 172˝ of black binding, and bind using your favorite method.

I chose to bind *Geese* with a wide black binding. The extra width in black adds a bit of formality, making it a nice piece of art to hang over the fireplace in my living room.

To make the wide binding, I cut the strips 3˝ wide. To sew it on, I used the edge of my walking foot for the seam allowance, which is about ⅜˝–½˝ rather than the standard ¼˝.

Quilting

Layer and baste the quilt sandwich (page 63).

The abundance of negative space in this quilt top is a quilter's dream! It's the perfect size quilt to practice new ideas. In this version, the geese are launched into space, leaving a vapor trail across the quilt. Use your imagination to see how far the geese can pop off the quilt.

FALL

QUILT: 25″ × 38″

Design note: I like the orderly look of the leaves on the right-hand side of this tree, but on the left I thought the leaves should go rogue, like a real tree does. Before gluing the leaves to the quilt top, experiment with placement to see if you can come up with something you like better.

Methods: Standard Freezer-Paper and Fabric Preparation (page 21), The Stitching Process (page 35), Appliqué on a Pieced Block (page 58)

FABRICS

FALL: made by Jenifer Dick, quilted by Angela Walters

APPLIQUÉ:
- 27 scraps (3″ × 3″ minimum) of gray prints in a variety of values
- Scrap (3″ × 6″ minimum) of gold print
- Scrap (6″ × 6″ minimum) of gold solid
- Scrap (4″ × 13″ minimum) of gray solid

BACKGROUND:
- ⅔ yard yellow solid
- 1 yard white solid (43″ wide)

BACKING:
- 1 yard white

BATTING:
- 30″ × 43″

BINDING:
- ⅜ yard white

APPLIQUÉ SUPPLIES:
- See Tools and Supplies (page 8).

Background

Starch the background fabrics with the desired amount of starch.

From yellow, cut 1 rectangle 19½˝ × 21˝.

From white, cut 3 strips 3½˝ × width of fabric and 1 piece 12˝ × 25½˝.

To create the sunset behind the tree, stitch and flip the corners to create a shape that is somewhat round. To do this, with the left-over white background fabric, cut a large triangle from a 12″ square. Lay it over the top right corner of the yellow rectangle to make sure it will cover the entire corner.

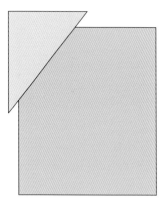

Note where the edge of the triangle is, and turn it so you can sew it onto the yellow rectangle. Press the seam allowances to the outside after sewing and trim the yellow from behind.

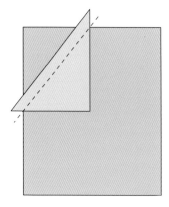

Continue around the yellow rectangle, using different sizes and angles of triangles until you're happy with the shape.

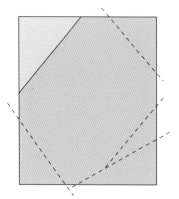

Trim the shape to 19½″ × 21″, or as close to this size as you can.

Once the center is done, add the borders. Measure the center from top to bottom. Cut a 3½″ strip to this length. Sew the cut strip to the right-hand side of the block and press the seam allowances toward the block. Measure again from side to side and add the next strip. Cut the strip and sew it to the bottom of the block. Continue with the remaining 2 sides, adding borders Log Cabin style. The block will be about 25½″ × 27″.

Sew the 12″ × 25½″ white piece to the bottom of the block. Press.

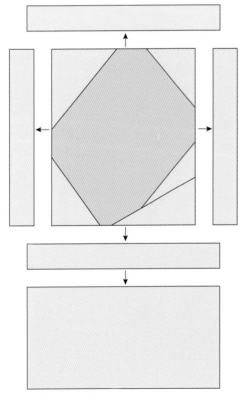

Quilt assembly diagram

Appliqué

Using the leaf and tree trunk patterns (below and on pattern pullout page P1), prepare 27 gray print leaves, 3 gold solid leaves, 2 gold print leaves, and a gray tree trunk, using the standard freezer-paper method.

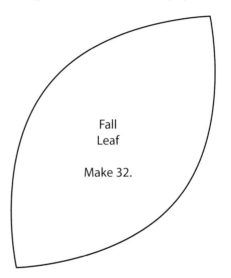

Fall
Leaf

Make 32.

Enlarge the placement diagram by 400% (page 115). Lay out the full-size placement diagram on a worktable with the quilt top centered on top of it. Glue each leaf and the tree trunk on the quilt top matching the leaves with the diagram. If you have trouble seeing through the quilt top, use a lightbox or glass-top table to help you see.

Once the quilt top is prepared, roll the ends to fit in the machine as you are appliquéing. Appliqué the shapes using invisible thread and a zigzag stitch. Reglue right away any shapes that come undone during the process. Remove the freezer paper and press.

Placement
diagram

Quilting

Layer and baste the quilt sandwich (page 63).

Quilt tightly around each leaf and the trunk, making them pop off the quilt. Stitch flames in the yellow to reinforce the sunset idea or fill it up with more leaves to make it seem as though it is part of the tree. Make dense swirls in the background that appear to be blowing the leaves off the tree.

Binding

Prepare 145˝ of white binding, and bind using your favorite method.

The Modern Appliqué Workbook

STAR BRIGHT

QUILT: 66″ × 66″ • BLOCK: 16½″ × 16½″

Design note: *Star Bright* takes advantage of all the fun, bright modern geometric fabrics available. A geometric is a simple shape: circle, square, polka dot, zigzag, and so on. Also look for shapes that aren't necessarily geometric (such as flowers) but are lined up in straight rows, giving the illusion of a geometric print.

Methods: Standard Freezer-Paper and Fabric Preparation (page 21), Press Registration Marks (page 22), Layered Patterns (page 53), The Stitching Process (page 35), Tip: Plan Ahead (page 39)

FABRICS

STAR BRIGHT:
made by
Jenifer Dick,
quilted by
Angela Walters

APPLIQUÉ:

- 1 yard medium gray solid or a mixture of gray solids, each at least 10″ × 10″, to total 1 yard, for circles
- Scraps (15″ × 15″ minimum) of 9 geometric prints in bright rainbow colors
- Scraps (15″ × 15″ minimum) of 9 solids that coordinate with the geometric prints
- 5″ charm squares of 9 contrasting prints for the stars

BACKGROUND:

- 3¼ yards of light gray solid or a mixture of light and medium gray solids to total 3¼ yards, with each piece being at least 18″ × 18″
- 1 fat quarter (18″ × 22″) each of 4 orange solids in any value

BACKING:

- 4¼ yards light gray

BATTING:

- 71″ × 71″

BINDING:

- ⅝ yard of light gray or leftover strips for piecing (see Binding, page 66)

APPLIQUÉ SUPPLIES:

- See Tools and Supplies (page 8).

Background

From gray solids, cut 12 squares 18″ × 18″.

From each orange solid fat quarter, cut 1 square 18″ × 18″.

Starch the lightest orange square and 8 of the gray squares with the desired amount of starch. Press the starched squares in half both vertically and horizontally to create registration marks.

Appliqué

Using the patterns (see pattern pullout page P2), prepare 10 appliqué shapes per block. Each block needs the following:

> 1 gray 8″ finished circle
>
> 1 contrasting center star
>
> 4 print *or* solid large wedges
>
> 4 print *or* solid small wedges

For each block, determine which combinations of colors you want. The bottom layer—the circle—is always gray. Other than that, you have freedom to mix and match the prints, solids, and contrasting colors. I chose to keep the same or a similar color family per block—red print with red solid, orange print with cheddar solid, and so on. Experiment with mixing up the colors or using 2 prints together in a single block to see if you like the effect better.

> **Tip**
>
> Because of the complex layering and fabric combinations, I made a block at a time rather than preparing all 90 appliqué shapes at once. This allowed me to concentrate on the block in front of me, keeping things from getting confused.

Once the 10 shapes are prepared for the block, lay out the full-size placement sheet (see pattern pullout page P2) on the worktable in front of you. Place the shapes on top of the diagram, starting with the bottom layer, then the circle, and building up from there, with the star centered on top. Once they are all perfectly aligned, glue the shapes together. When dry, transfer the appliqué to the background square and center it, using the pressed registration marks. Glue it to the background.

Before you start appliquéing, determine a path that will give you the fewest starts and stops. Then appliqué the design in place. Remove the freezer paper and press. Trim the block to 17″ square. Repeat to make 9 blocks: 8 blocks with a gray background and 1 block with an orange background.

> **Tip**
>
> To avoid having overlapping layers of freezer paper, you can glue in place and appliqué the bottom gray circle first. Then, remove the freezer-paper template. Next, place all the wedges on top and appliqué them in place. Then, remove those freezer-paper templates. Last, place the star on top of the wedges and appliqué in place. Finish the block by removing the star freezer-paper shapes. Removing the freezer paper as you go rather than waiting until the entire block is sewn makes it easier to remove the freezer paper from this block. However, it is also possible to remove the freezer paper all at once after it's sewn, which is what I did.

Assembly

On a design wall, place the 16 blocks in 4 rows of 4. Refer to the quilt photo for a possible configuration, or experiment with others. Stand back and make sure the appliqué colors are spread out evenly over the quilt top and the orange blocks are where you want them. Sew the rows together, pressing the seam allowances in opposite directions from row to row after each seam is sewn. Join the 4 rows and press.

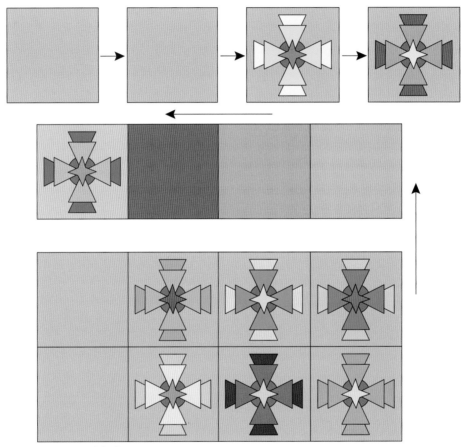

Quilt assembly diagram

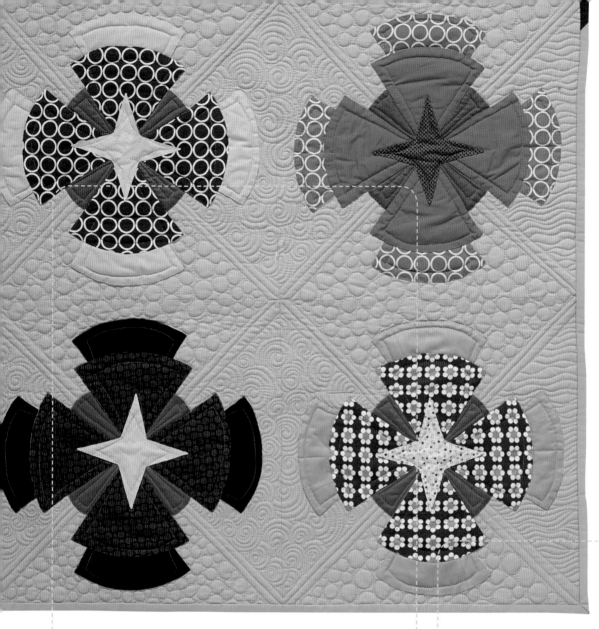

Quilting

Layer and baste the quilt sandwich (page 63).

Star Bright is designed with a lot of negative space for creative quilting—the perfect place to showcase your quilting skills. In this version, the appliqué blocks have been quilted to look like they are on point when they are really not. The open gray spaces are filled with contrasting wavy lines, and the open orange spaces are filled with swirls. The quilting is so exuberant it almost steals the show!

Binding

The colorful and playful nature of this quilt makes it a natural for a fun binding. I randomly pieced 2½˝-wide leftover strips of the appliqué fabric on the diagonal, to make about 290˝ of binding.

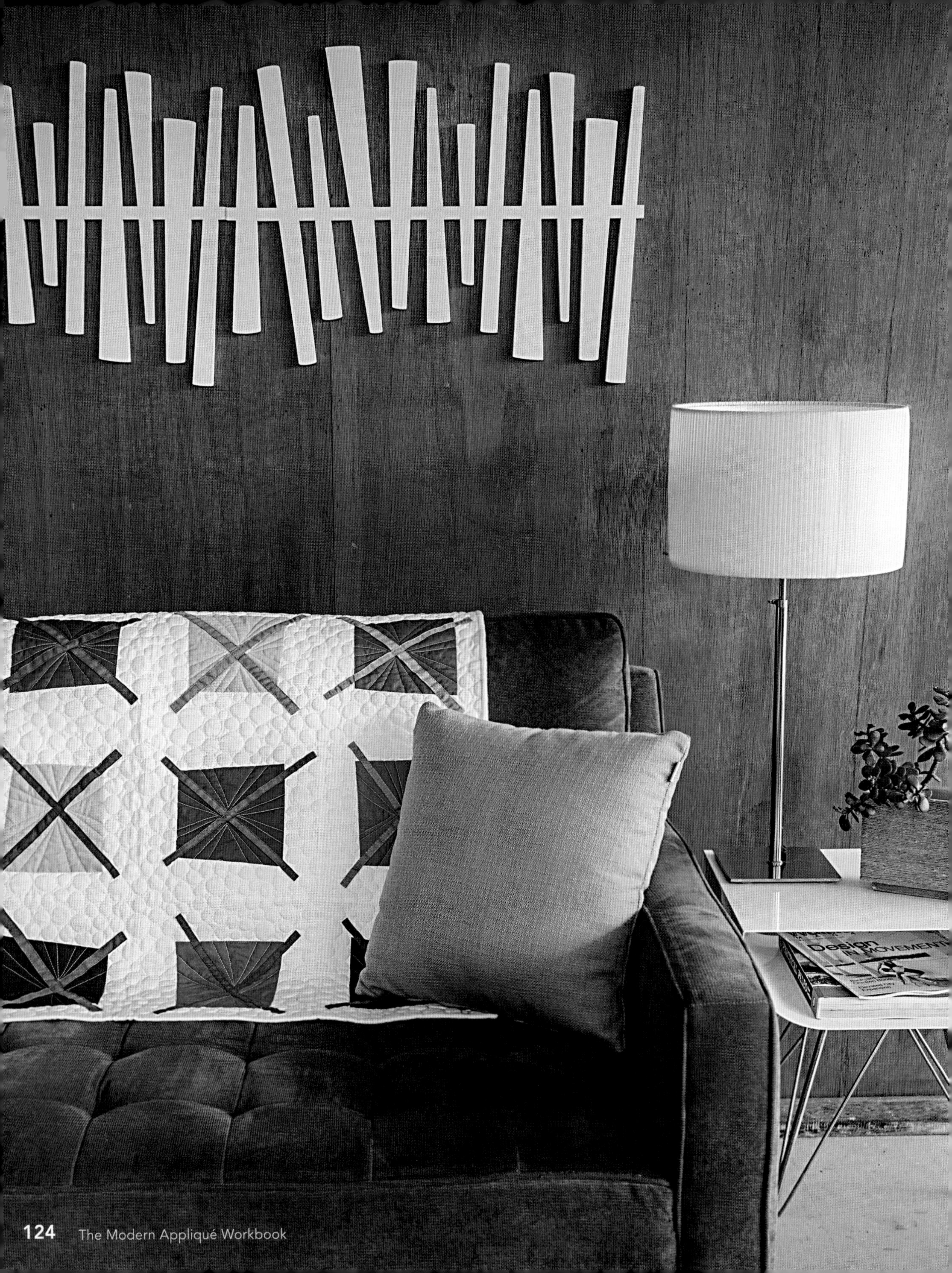
Design
IN MOVEMENT

KISSES

QUILT: 36″ × 45″ • BLOCK: 9″ × 9″

Design note: When collecting the blues for *Kisses*, don't worry about finding an exact gradation of colors. It's okay to have a mixture of colors, but just make sure the five blues have different values.

Methods: Standard Freezer-Paper and Fabric Preparation (page 21), Straight-Grain Tape (page 59), Single Straight-Line Stitch (page 48), Appliqué on a Pieced Block (page 58)

FABRICS

KISSES: made by Jenifer Dick, quilted by Angela Walters

APPLIQUÉ:
- 1 fat quarter (18″ × 22″) medium gray
- 1 fat quarter (18″ × 22″) medium-dark gray

BLOCKS:
Starch the block fabrics with the desired amount of starch.

- 1 fat quarter (18″ × 22″) *each of* 5 shades of blue, light to dark
- 1¾ yards white

BACKING:
- 1½ yards white

BATTING:
- 42″ × 51″

BINDING:
- ½ yard white

APPLIQUÉ SUPPLIES:
- See Tools and Supplies (page 8).

Background

From each blue fat quarter, cut 4 squares 6″ × 6″.

From white, cut:

  40 rectangles 3″ × 7½″

  40 rectangles 3″ × 10″

From each of the 20 blue squares, refer to the diagram and trim off the sides on the diagonal, starting from the outer bottom corners and angling in slightly to create a trapezoid—make sure each side is cut at a different angle so the shape isn't a symmetrical trapezoid. Stack a few at a time or cut each individually for more variety.

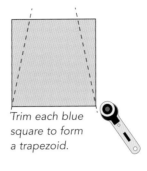

Trim each blue square to form a trapezoid.

Sew a 3″ × 7″ white rectangle to each side of a blue trapezoid. The sides will be on the bias after sewing, so be careful when pressing. Press the seam allowances toward the blue trapezoids. Trim the top and the bottom of the unit flush with the blue fabric.

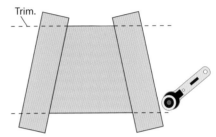

Trim.

Sew the side strips to the trapezoid.

Center and sew a 3″ × 10″ rectangle to the top and bottom of the block. Press the seam allowances toward the blue trapezoid.

Repeat to make 20 blocks, using all the blue trapezoids and the white rectangles.

Sew the top and bottom strips to finish the block.

Tip

Don't square up the block at this point. There will be shrinkage during the appliqué process so you want the extra size for squaring up after the blocks are done.

Appliqué

Prepare 40 straight-grain tape strips 10″ long (see Straight-Grain Tape, page 59). Make a variety of ⅜″ and ½″ strips in both the gray and medium-gray fabrics to mix and match as desired. Turn each short end under and glue. Stack according to size and color. Glue the strips on the blue section of each block in an X. The X's don't have to be identical from block to block. Mix and match skinny and wide strips or keep skinny with skinny and wide with wide. I kept the colors consistent on each block while mixing up the widths.

Sew each strip down along the outer edge using matching thread and a straight-line stitch. Or the appliqué lines can be slightly wavy for a more casual look.

After the appliqué is finished, trim each block to 9½″ × 9½″ and press.

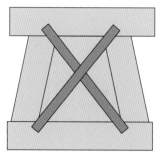

Glue each strip to form an X on the block. Sew close to the edge in either straight or wavy lines, depending on the desired look.

Finished Kisses block

Assembly

On a design wall, lay out the blocks in 5 rows of 4 blocks each. Spread out the shades of blue across the quilt top, but it doesn't have to be perfectly balanced. Also, rotate the blocks so they aren't all facing the same direction. This gives the illusion that you did more piecing than you actually did.

Sew the rows together and press seam allowances in opposite directions from row to row as you go along. Join the rows to finish the quilt top. Press each seam after it is sewn.

Quilt assembly diagram

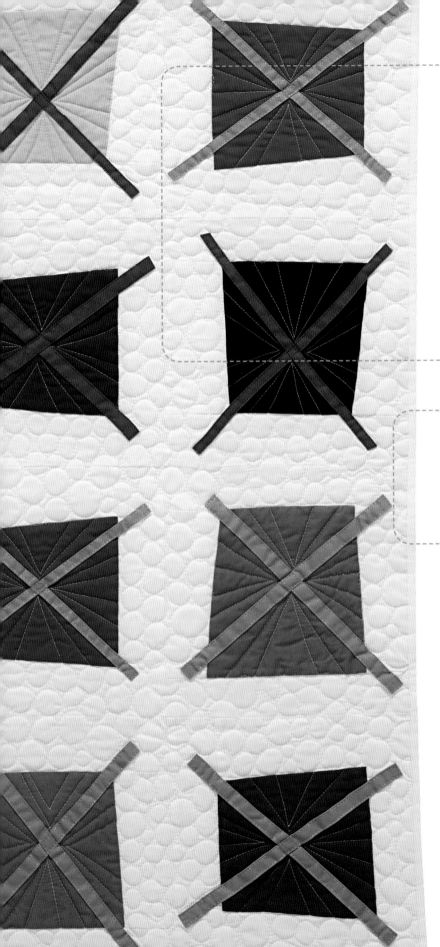

Quilting

Layer and baste the quilt sandwich (page 63).

The blue squares are filled with straight lines radiating from the center, while the appliquéd X's remain unquilted. Circles fill in the white background in stark contrast to the squares and X's.

Binding

Prepare 185″ of white binding, and bind using your favorite method.

FISH

QUILT: Approximately 17″ × 21″

Design note: I found a print for the background in the exact colors to match the batiks for the fish. If you can't find a stripe you like, you can either piece a panel to use as the background or use a solid pale blue.

Methods: Standard Freezer-Paper and Fabric Preparation (page 21), Press Registration Marks (page 22), Bias Tape (page 59), The Stitching Process (page 35)

FABRICS

FISH: made by Jenifer Dick, quilted by Angela Walters

APPLIQUÉ:
- 1 fat quarter (18″ × 21″) blue batik

BACKGROUND:
- 1 fat quarter (18″ × 21″) aqua stripe

BACKING:
- ⅝ yard blue batik

BATTING:
- 22″ × 26″

BINDING:
- ⅓ yard blue batik

APPLIQUÉ SUPPLIES:
- See Tools and Supplies (page 8).

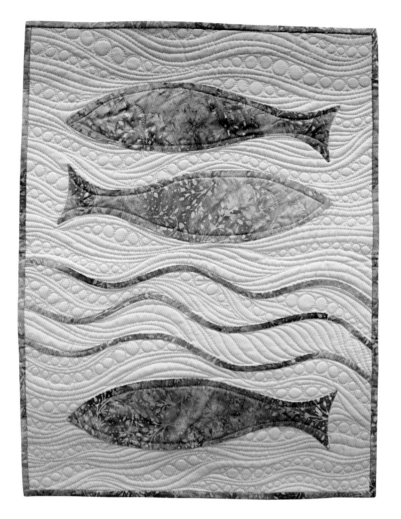

Background

Starch the aqua stripe background fabric with the desired amount of starch. Press in half both vertically and horizontally to create registration marks.

Bias Tape

From the fat quarter of batik, cut 3 strips on the bias ⅜″ wide and prepare 3 finished bias strips ¼″ × about 25″.

Remember you will need to cut the 3 bias strips and the 3 fish shapes out of a single fat quarter. Plan it out to make the most of the fabric.

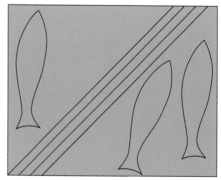

From the fat quarter, first cut the bias strips and then the 3 fish shapes.

Appliqué

Using the pattern (see pattern pullout page P1), prepare 3 fish from the remaining fat quarter fabric. There is no need to reverse a fish.

Once the bias tape and fish shapes are done, lay them out on the starched background. Refer to the quilt photo or place them in another configuration you like. Make sure a fish goes the opposite direction from the other 2. Glue all the fish in place.

On the ironing board, press the bias strips into waves. To do this, gently pull the strip in the direction you want it to go with your left hand as you press the tape with your right. Make the waves as tight as you can without bunching up the bias strip. It will loosen slightly as it cools.

Place the 3 strips on the background and glue them in place. Appliqué the shapes and bias tape using invisible thread and a zigzag stitch. Remove the freezer paper from the fish, and press. The bias tape will draw up slightly as you appliqué it down. This is normal. After you remove the freezer paper from the fish, press while the fabric is still damp, and the puckers will flatten out. Press until dry.

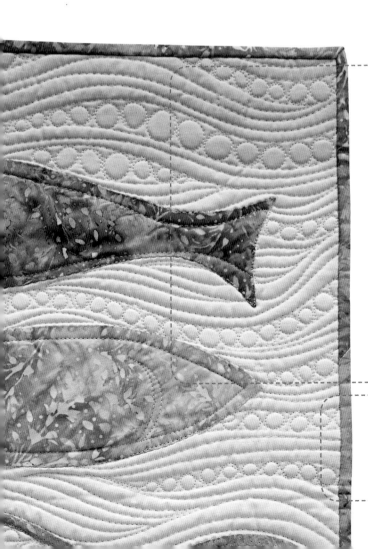

Quilting

Layer and baste the quilt sandwich (page 63).

Fish is quilted with long, wavy lines that follow the design set by the bias tape. Between the lines, bubbles appear, making the fish look as though they are swimming under water. The fish themselves are quilted sparsely— only enough to define the shape. Heavy quilting on the fish won't show up on the print of the batik fabric, so a little quilting is just enough.

Binding

Prepare 100″ of blue binding, and bind using your favorite method.

Resources

FABRIC AND QUILTMAKING SUPPLIES

Most tools and supplies mentioned in this book are available at your local quilt shop or online.

Thread
Superior Threads
superiorthreads.com

Sulky
sulky.com

Washing
Retayne (dye fixative); **Synthrapol** (sizing and dye remover)
prochemicalanddye.com

Orvus Paste Soap or Quilt Soap
Check local quilt shops or farm supply stores.

Fabrics
Pink Chalk Fabrics
pinkchalkfabrics.com

Marmalade Fabrics
marmaladefabrics.com

INSPIRATION

Books
Barbara Brackman's Encyclopedia of Appliqué by Barbara Brackman

Mastering Machine Appliqué: The Complete Guide by Harriet Hargrave

Blogs
Quilting: Quilting Is My Therapy by Angela Walters
quiltingismytherapy.com

More on modern appliqué: Esch House Quilts by Debbie Grifka
eschhousequilts.blogspot.com

About the Author

Jenifer Dick began quilting in 1993 when, on a whim, she signed up for a beginning quiltmaking class. From that first stitch she was hooked. In 2001 she discovered appliqué, and it changed her quilting life. She has been speaking to guilds and teaching appliqué to quiltmakers ever since. She is the author of 4 quilt books on topics from traditional to modern, and her work has been published in many other books and magazines. Jenifer lives in Harrisonville, Missouri, with her husband and 3 children. Follow her on her blog, 42 Quilts, at 42quilts.com.

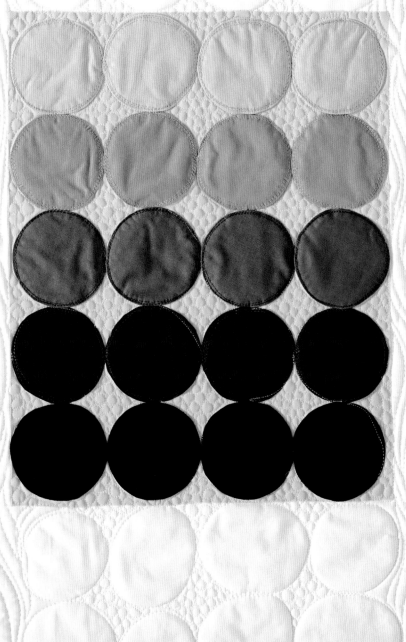

Photo by Tela Gough, telabethphotography.com

stashBOOKS®

fabric arts for a handmade lifestyle

If you're craving beautiful authenticity in a time of mass-production...Stash Books is for you. Stash Books is a line of how-to books celebrating fabric arts for a handmade lifestyle. Backed by C&T Publishing's solid reputation for quality, Stash Books will inspire you with contemporary designs, clear and simple instructions, and engaging photography.

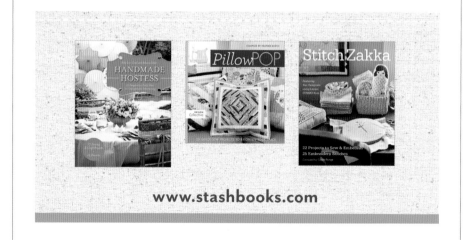

www.stashbooks.com